T0198952

An Analysis of

Janet L. Abu-Lughod's

Before European Hegemony

William R. Day, Jr.

Published by Macat International Ltd
24:13 Coda Centre, 189 Munster Road, London SW6 6AW.

Distributed exclusively by Routledge
2 Park Square, Milton Park, Abingdon, Oxon OX14 4RN
711 Third Avenue, New York, NY 10017, USA

Routledge is an imprint of the Taylor & Francis Group, an informa business

www.macat.com
info@macat.com

Cataloguing in Publication Data
A catalogue record for this book is available from the British Library.
Library of Congress Cataloguing-in-Publication Data is available upon request.
Cover illustration: Etienne Gilfillan

ISBN 978-1-912302-41-3 (hardback)
ISBN 978-1-912128-76-1 (paperback)
ISBN 978-1-912281-29-9 (e-book)

Notice
The information in this book is designed to orientate readers of the work under analysis,
to elucidate and contextualise its key ideas and themes, and to aid in the development
of critical thinking skills. It is not meant to be used, nor should it be used, as a
substitute for original thinking or in place of original writing or research. References and
notes are provided for informational purposes and their presence does not constitute
endorsement of the information or opinions therein. This book is presented solely for
educational purposes. It is sold on the understanding that the publisher is not engaged
to provide any scholarly advice. The publisher has made every effort to ensure that
this book is accurate and up-to-date, but makes no warranties or representations with
regard to the completeness or reliability of the information it contains. The information
and the opinions provided herein are not guaranteed or warranted to produce particular
results and may not be suitable for students of every ability. The publisher shall not be
liable for any loss, damage or disruption arising from any errors or omissions, or from
the use of this book, including, but not limited to, special, incidental, consequential or
other damages caused, or alleged to have been caused, directly or indirectly, by the
information contained within.

CONTENTS

THE MACAT LIBRARY

The Macat Library is a series of unique academic explorations of seminal works in the humanities and social sciences – books and papers that have had a significant and widely recognised impact on their disciplines. It has been created to serve as much more than just a summary of what lies between the covers of a great book. It illuminates and explores the influences on, ideas of, and impact of that book. Our goal is to offer a learning resource that encourages critical thinking and fosters a better, deeper understanding of important ideas.

Each publication is divided into three Sections: Influences, Ideas, and Impact. Each Section has four Modules. These explore every important facet of the work, and the responses to it.

This Section-Module structure makes a Macat Library book easy to use, but it has another important feature. Because each Macat book is written to the same format, it is possible (and encouraged!) to cross-reference multiple Macat books along the same lines of inquiry or research. This allows the reader to open up interesting interdisciplinary pathways.

To further aid your reading, lists of glossary terms and people mentioned are included at the end of this book (these are indicated by an asterisk [*] throughout) – as well as a list of works cited.

Macat has worked with the University of Cambridge to identify the elements of critical thinking and understand the ways in which six different skills combine to enable effective thinking.
Three allow us to fully understand a problem; three more give us the tools to solve it. Together, these six skills make up the **PACIER** model of critical thinking. They are:

ANALYSIS – understanding how an argument is built
EVALUATION – exploring the strengths and weaknesses of an argument
INTERPRETATION – understanding issues of meaning

CREATIVE THINKING – coming up with new ideas and fresh connections
PROBLEM-SOLVING – producing strong solutions
REASONING – creating strong arguments

To find out more, visit **WWW.MACAT.COM.**

CRITICAL THINKING AND *BEFORE EUROPEAN HEGEMONY*

Primary critical thinking skill: CREATIVE THINKING
Secondary critical thinking skill: INTERPRETATION

The modern vision of the world as one dominated by one or more superpowers begs the question of how best to understand the world-system that existed before the rise of the first modern powers.

Janet Abu-Lughod's solution to this problem, in this highly influential work, is that before European hegemony, a predominantly insular, agrarian world was dominated by groups of mercantile city-states that traded with one another on equal terms across a series of interlocking areas of influence. In this reading of history, China and Japan, the kingdoms of India, Muslim caliphates, the Byzantine Empire and European maritime republics alike enjoyed no absolute dominance over their neighbours and commercial partners – and the egalitarian international trading network that they built endured until European advances in weaponry and ship types introduced radical instability to the system.

Abu-Lughod's portrait of a more balanced world is a masterpiece of synthesis driven by one highly creative idea: her world system of interlocking spheres of influence quite literally connected masses of evidence together in new ways. A triumph of fine critical thinking.

ABOUT THE AUTHOR OF THE ORIGINAL WORK

American urban sociologist and historian **Janet Abu-Lughod** was born Janet Lippman in 1928 and took the name she is known by when she married Palestinian scholar Ibrahim Abu-Lughod in 1951. She accompanied him to Cairo, where she taught and did research that led to her writing an acclaimed history of the city. Her most famous work, Before European Hegemony, demonstrates that the modern world-system grew out of an older, more balanced medieval one in which no one area dominated others in the way that Europe later would. Abu-Lughod went on to write well-received books about the three largest American cities, New York, Los Angeles, and Chicago. She died in 2013 at the age of 85.

ABOUT THE AUTHOR OF THE ANALYSIS

Dr William R. Day holds a PhD in medieval economic history from the University of Cambridge. He is currently a researcher at the Fitzwilliam Museum at the University of Cambridge, where he works on the Medieval European Coinage Project.

ABOUT MACAT

GREAT WORKS FOR CRITICAL THINKING

Macat is focused on making the ideas of the world's great thinkers accessible and comprehensible to everybody, everywhere, in ways that promote the development of enhanced critical thinking skills.

It works with leading academics from the world's top universities to produce new analyses that focus on the ideas and the impact of the most influential works ever written across a wide variety of academic disciplines. Each of the works that sit at the heart of its growing library is an enduring example of great thinking. But by setting them in context – and looking at the influences that shaped their authors, as well as the responses they provoked – Macat encourages readers to look at these classics and game-changers with fresh eyes. Readers learn to think, engage and challenge their ideas, rather than simply accepting them.

'Macat offers an amazing first-of-its-kind tool for interdisciplinary learning and research. Its focus on works that transformed their disciplines and its rigorous approach, drawing on the world's leading experts and educational institutions, opens up a world-class education to anyone.'

Andreas Schleicher
Director for Education and Skills, Organisation for Economic
Co-operation and Development

'Macat is taking on some of the major challenges in university education … They have drawn together a strong team of active academics who are producing teaching materials that are novel in the breadth of their approach.'

Prof Lord Broers,
former Vice-Chancellor of the University of Cambridge

'The Macat vision is exceptionally exciting. It focuses upon new modes of learning which analyse and explain seminal texts which have profoundly influenced world thinking and so social and economic development. It promotes the kind of critical thinking which is essential for any society and economy. This is the learning of the future.'

Rt Hon Charles Clarke, former UK Secretary of State for Education

'The Macat analyses provide immediate access to the critical conversation surrounding the books that have shaped their respective discipline, which will make them an invaluable resource to all of those, students and teachers, working in the field.'

Professor William Tronzo, University of California at San Diego

WAYS IN TO THE TEXT

KEY POINTS

- Janet Abu-Lughod (1928–2013) was an urban sociologist (a scholar of the social structures of towns and cities) and historian from the United States. She worked in the US and in Cairo and finished her career as a professor at the New School of Social Research in New York.

- Her book *Before European Hegemony* (1989) examines the behavior and development of large-scale socioeconomic systems in Europe, the Middle East, and Asia during the thirteenth and fourteenth centuries; it focuses on the way that these systems interacted and the key role that cities played in their interactions.

- *Before European Hegemony* describes a world in which the European socioeconomic system had not yet achieved dominance over those of the Middle East and Asia but, rather, interacted with them on more or less equal terms.

Who Was *Janet Abu-Lughod?*

Janet Abu-Lughod, the author of *Before European Hegemony: The World-System A.D. 1250–1350* (1989), was born Janet Lippman in the American state of New Jersey in 1928. After gaining her undergraduate and graduate degrees from the University of Chicago (in 1947 and 1950), she received her PhD from the University of Massachusetts Amherst in 1966. She taught at the University of

Illinois, the American University in Cairo, Smith College, and Northwestern University before joining the New School of Social Research in New York as professor of sociology and historical studies in 1987. She retired in 1998 and died in 2013.

In 1951, Janet married the Palestinian political science scholar and activist Ibrahim Abu-Lughod; their careers were to be linked. While Ibrahim worked in Egypt for the United Nations cultural body UNESCO (the United Nations Educational, Scientific and Cultural Organization), Janet taught at the American University in Cairo—the city that was the subject both of her PhD thesis and of a book-length history published in 1971.[1]

In 1966, Ibrahim and Janet Abu-Lughod returned to North America, where their careers followed similar paths. Janet Abu-Lughod built her reputation as a leading urban sociologist with a string of groundbreaking books.[2]

What Does *Before European Hegemony* Say?

Janet Abu-Lughod's *Before European Hegemony: The World-System A.D. 1250–1350* describes the "world-system"*—a socioeconomic system larger than that of a single state—of the thirteenth and fourteenth centuries.

The structure of any world-system usually hinges on the distribution of wealth and the division of labor between "sub-systems" (in this case, the overlapping systems of Europe, the Middle East, and Asia). Abu-Lughod views the world-system of the thirteenth and fourteenth centuries in terms of "interaction networks" in which these overlapping sub-systems interacted on more or less equal terms.

Another characteristic of the system, she writes, is that interaction between sub-systems occurred through a network of "world cities."* Around the middle of the fourteenth century, the medieval world-system broke down and gradually evolved into the modern world-system. Unlike the system that preceded it, this system had a single core that dominated other parts of the system. At first, this core included only Western Europe; later it extended across the Atlantic to North America. Scholars describe the other sub-systems within the wider system as the semi-periphery (comprising developing countries) and the periphery (made up of lesser-developed countries).

Before European Hegemony helped to promote world-systems analysis, a discipline drawing on the aims and methods of world history* and sociology, as a distinct field of study. Research in the field first focused on the development of the modern world-system from the sixteenth century onward, following the influential American historical sociologist Immanuel Wallerstein* and his multi-volume study *The Modern World-System* (1974–2011).[3]

However, whereas Wallerstein treated the modern world-system with its "particular hierarchical structure" as the first such system—a definition that seemed to exclude the possibility of structurally different types of organization—Abu-Lughod argues that the modern world-system evolved from an earlier world-system. In the earlier system, the European sub-system was one of three interdependent, and fairly equal, core regions. Interaction between the different sub-systems occurred through a network of "world cities."

When it first appeared in 1989, *Before European Hegemony* drew strong reactions from scholars working across a range of disciplines, and in the process stimulated debate about the nature and structure of world-systems. The book's influence has perhaps been greatest in university classrooms, where it has secured a place on undergraduate and graduate syllabuses as a useful teaching text. The work engages with the theories of important thinkers such as the German economist and social theorist Karl Marx,* the Belgian historian Henri Pirenne,* and the pioneering German sociologist Max Weber.* It explores perennial questions about the origins of capitalism* (the economic and social model dominant in the West and across much of the developing world), the revival of cities in Europe, and the distinctive character of the Western city. The book's multidisciplinary approach and broad geographic scale make it adaptable to a variety of teaching contexts.

Why Does *Before European Hegemony* Matter?

In geographic terms, Janet Abu-Lughod's *Before European Hegemony* covers the entire Eurasian continent and part of North Africa, considering geographic regions in Europe, the Middle East, and Asia that are usually studied by separate sets of specialists. Conducting comparisons over such a vast area, Abu-Lughod exploited her expertise in urban studies to focus on a common denominator—world cities. Examining the medieval world-system through the prism of key cities that functioned as points of contact between different parts of the system, she finds that the trade that moved through these cities set the conditions for production and for the organization of labor in these cities' hinterlands,* determining the shape of the entire system.

This decision to focus on world cities was a brilliant piece of intuition that allowed her to compare distant parts of the system on similar terms while limiting her research to manageable proportions.

Abu-Lughod further recognized that the interpretation of data depends as much on the observer, and what he or she brings to the observation, as it does on the data itself. In other words, she recognized the importance of considering the medieval world-system from a variety of perspectives. This led to a thoroughly multidisciplinary approach to her research. While *Before European Hegemony* is essentially a work of medieval history and economic history, it draws on disciplines such as sociology, urban studies, and international development (the study of developing nations). Each discipline has its own concerns and traditions that influence scholars working within it. Specialists in different disciplines sometimes view the same information differently. So research that cuts across disciplinary lines opens up different ways of seeing and understanding.

Although Abu-Lughod familiarized herself with research in different disciplines by reading widely, she realized that her grasp of new material would always be superficial compared with the knowledge of specialists.

Abu-Lughod's interest in considering problems from multiple perspectives went beyond simply crossing the boundaries of academic disciplines. For her, it was important to take into account not only the perspectives of dominant groups in Western culture but also the perspectives of "subaltern"* groups—that is, the more marginalized parts of society. She sought to present a balanced account of the medieval world-system that incorporated the interpretations of the victims and the vanquished along with those of the victors.

The methodology that Abu-Lughod adopted in her research for *Before European Hegemony* may serve as a model for approaching any complex problems, especially those that involve comparative study. To limit her project to manageable proportions, she focused on the common denominator of key cities and their place in the international trade network. To open up new ways of understanding the available information, she read extensively in other disciplines and considered as many different perspectives as possible.

NOTES

1   Janet L. Abu-Lughod, "The Ecology of Cairo, Egypt: A Comparative Study Using Factor Analysis" (PhD diss., University of Massachusetts Amherst, 1966); Janet L. Abu-Lughod, *Cairo: 1001 Years of the City Victorious* (Princeton, NJ: Princeton University Press, 1971).

2   In addition to her book on Cairo, see Janet L. Abu-Lughod, *Rabat: Urban Apartheid in Morocco* (Princeton, NJ: Princeton University Press, 1980); Janet L. Abu-Lughod, *Changing Cities: Urban Sociology* (Glenview, IL: HarperCollins, 1991); Janet L. Abu-Lughod, *New York, Chicago, Los Angeles: America's Global Cities* (Minneapolis: University of Minnesota Press, 1999); Janet L. Abu-Lughod, *Race, Space, and Riots in Chicago, New York, and Los Angeles* (Oxford: Oxford University Press, 2007).

3   Immanuel M. Wallerstein, *Capitalist Agriculture and the Origins of the European World-Economy in the Sixteenth Century*, vol. 1 of *The Modern World-System* (New York: Academic Press, 1974); Immanuel M. Wallerstein, *Mercantilism and the Consolidation of the European World-Economy, 1600–1750*, vol. 2 of *The Modern World-System* (New York: Academic Press, 1980); Immanuel M. Wallerstein, *The Second Era of Great Expansion of the Capitalist World-Economy, 1730–1840s*, vol. 3 of *The Modern World-System* (London: Academic Press, 1989); Immanuel M. Wallerstein, *Centrist Liberalism Triumphant, 1789–1914*, vol. 4 of *The Modern World-System* (Berkeley: University of California Press, 2011).

SECTION 1
INFLUENCES

MODULE 1
THE AUTHOR AND THE HISTORICAL CONTEXT

KEY POINTS

- *Before European Hegemony* describes the international trade network across Europe, the Middle East, and Asia in the period between 1250 and 1350 in the context of world-systems analysis*—a field of research that inquires into world history* and social change beyond the level of the nation-state.

- The text both extends Abu-Lughod's enduring interest in cities and carries her previous work in new directions.

- Abu-Lughod's early work on Cairo and her marriage to a Palestinian political scientist helped to give her scholarly work more of a global approach.

Why Read this Text?

Janet Abu-Lughod's *Before European Hegemony: The World-System A.D. 1250–1350* (1989) is a study of the international trade network, or "world-system," of the thirteenth and fourteenth centuries.

While world-systems are large-scale social and economic systems generally based on the hierarchical division of labor among regions, Abu-Lughod views the Eurasian world-system of the Middle Ages in terms of "interaction networks."[1] The medieval system, she argues, was made up of eight interdependent sub-systems that extended across three core regions in Europe, the Middle East, and Asia—an approach differing from the orthodox belief that one sub-system or region dominated in any given period. For Abu-Lughod, the core regions in the overall system interacted on more or less

> ❝ This book ... takes the position that in terms of time, the century between AD 1250 and 1350 constituted a fulcrum or critical 'turning point' in world history, and in terms of space, the Middle East heartland region, linking the eastern Mediterranean with the Indian Ocean, constituted a geographic fulcrum in which the East and West were then roughly balanced. ❞
>
> Janet Abu-Lughod, *Before European Hegemony: The World-System A.D. 1250–1350*

equal terms through an extensive network of "world cities."*

Before European Hegemony is notable in being the only major study of international trade networks during the Middle Ages that devotes equal attention to Europe, the Middle East, and Asia. The book's mostly jargon-free presentation and the way that it engages with enduring questions about the rise of the West and the nature of world-systems have also made it a useful teaching text. Finally, its focus on major trading cities highlights the influence that those cities had on production and the organization of labor in the hinterlands* around them to make export possible.

The title of Abu-Lughod's book refers to a seminal, or groundbreaking, work by the American historical sociologist Immanuel Wallerstein,* a pioneer of world-systems analysis. In 1974, Wallerstein began to publish his multi-volume study titled *The Modern World-System*; the second volume appeared in 1980, and subsequent volumes were published in 1989 and 2011.[2] The modern world-system, according to Wallerstein, took shape in the sixteenth century as the first large-scale socioeconomic system of its kind. The countries of Western Europe and later North America made up the core of the system. Developing countries occupied the "semi-periphery," while lesser-developed countries made up the "periphery."

In her book, Abu-Lughod considers the earlier multi-centered world-system from which Wallerstein's modern system arose. In this way, she challenged both Wallerstein's conception of the modern world-system as the first such system and the implication that world-systems are necessarily hierarchical, with one part of the system dominating the others. She also sought to develop the main theme of the American historian William McNeill's* book *The Rise of the West* (1963),[3] a work focusing on the interaction between civilizations and the effect of Western civilization on other societies.

Author's Life

Abu-Lughod began her career as an urban sociologist (someone engaged in research on the social structure and functioning of cities and towns), demographer (someone conducting research on the statistics of things such as births and deaths that define changes in human populations), and planner (someone employed in the practical aspects of urban development). She subsequently studied economic and development planning, geography, and history.

Born Janet Lippman in the American state of New Jersey in 1928, she obtained undergraduate and graduate degrees from the University of Chicago (in 1947 and 1950) and a PhD from the University of Massachusetts Amherst (in 1966). She taught at the University of Illinois, the American University in Cairo, Smith College, Northwestern University, and finally, from 1987 to 1998, at the New School of Social Research in New York. In 1951, she married Ibrahim Abu-Lughod, a Palestinian political science scholar who taught at Smith College, McGill University, and Northwestern University. Following their divorce, Ibrahim Abu-Lughod returned to his native Palestine, dying there of a lung tumor in 2001; Janet Abu-Lughod remained in New York City until her death in 2013.[4]

Janet's marriage to Ibrahim Abu-Lughod influenced her work. Born in Palestine in 1929, Ibrahim left the region after the establishment of the state of Israel in 1948 and became a refugee in the United States, where he earned degrees from the University of Illinois and, in 1957, a PhD from Princeton University.[5] For the next 40 years, the careers of Janet and Ibrahim followed similar courses. While Ibrahim worked in Egypt with the United Nations cultural body UNESCO, Janet taught at the American University in Cairo, which was of significance in her career, as it was where she laid the groundwork not only for her PhD dissertation but also for her later book on the history of Cairo.[6]

On the couple's return to North America in the early 1960s, Janet continued her academic career at Smith College in Northampton, Massachusetts, where Ibrahim at that point began his. In 1966, Ibrahim took up a position at McGill University in Montreal before they both moved to Northwestern University in Evanston, Illinois, in 1967. We might assume that Janet's relationship with Ibrahim, as well as the time she spent in Egypt, helped her to consider European and world history in the thirteenth and fourteenth centuries from non-Western points of view.

Author's Background

In the 1960s, as Janet Abu-Lughod completed her PhD and began her teaching career, international affairs were dominated by the Cold War*—a long period of tension between the United States and its allies, and the communist Soviet Union* and its allies—and upheaval in the Middle East. Because of her marriage to Ibrahim Abu-Lughod—a Palestinian refugee, academic activist, and advocate of Palestinian liberation—and her own research interests, events in the Middle East clearly had a significant impact on her.

Both her PhD thesis and her first published work focused on Cairo.[7] Her close ties with the Middle East, both personally and intellectually, encouraged her to cast aside Western preconceptions about the Middle Ages and situate the history of Europe within a much broader context.

If contemporary events in the Middle East had any influence on her thinking as she planned her research agenda for *Before European Hegemony*, however, she never openly recognized it. She acknowledged only that her work on Cairo had led her to question both the Belgian historian Henri Pirenne's* thesis on the revival of European cities in the Middle Ages and the German sociologist Max Weber's* distinction between Western and Eastern cities.[8] Whereas Pirenne tied the growth of cities in Europe during the Middle Ages to the expansion of trade, Weber believed that it was citizenship and religion that gave European cities their distinctive character.

NOTES

1   Christopher Chase-Dunn et al., "In Memoriam: Janet L. Abu-Lughod's Contribution to World-Systems Research," *Journal of World-Systems Research* 20 (2014): 173–84.

2   Immanuel M. Wallerstein, *Capitalist Agriculture and the Origins of the European World-Economy in the Sixteenth Century*, vol. 1 of *The Modern World-System* (New York: Academic Press, 1974); *Mercantilism and the Consolidation of the European World-Economy, 1600–1750*, vol. 2 of *The Modern World-System* (New York: Academic Press, 1980).

3   William H. McNeill, *The Rise of the West: A History of the Human Community* (Chicago: University of Chicago Press, 1963).

4   Soraya Altorki, "Obituary: Janet L. Abu-Lughod (1928–2013)," *Al-Ahram* (Cairo), January 2, 2014.

5   Eric Pace, "Ibrahim Abu-Lughod, 72, Palestinian-American Scholar," *New York Times*, May 28, 2001; Edward Said, "Ibrahim Abu-Lughod," *Guardian*, June 12, 2001; Edward Said, "My Guru: Elegy for Ibrahim Abu-Lughod," *London Review of Books*, December 13, 2001; Ibrahim Abu-Lughod, "The Arab Rediscovery of Europe, 1800–1870" (PhD diss., Princeton University, 1957); Ibrahim Abu-Lughod, *The Arab Rediscovery of Europe: A Study in Cultural Encounters* (Princeton, NJ: Princeton University Press, 1963).

6   Janet L. Abu-Lughod, "The Ecology of Cairo, Egypt: A Comparative Study Using Factor Analysis" (PhD diss., University of Massachusetts Amherst, 1966); Janet L. Abu-Lughod, *Cairo: 1001 Years of the City Victorious* (Princeton, NJ: Princeton University Press, 1971).

7   Abu-Lughod, "The Ecology of Cairo"; Abu-Lughod, *Cairo: 1001 Years of the City Victorious*.

8   Janet L. Abu-Lughod, *Before European Hegemony: The World-System A.D. 1250–1350* (Oxford: Oxford University Press, 1989), ix–x.

MODULE 2
ACADEMIC CONTEXT

KEY POINTS

- *Before European Hegemony* drew inspiration from Immanuel Wallerstein's* work *The Modern World-System*, which describes the European-dominated world-system*—a socioeconomic organization larger than any single nation—that took shape around the year 1500.

- Abu-Lughod developed her ideas at a time when historians of the influential *Annales* school* took a "total history" approach, stressing both geographic and environmental factors and large-scale social and economic structures.

- While Abu-Lughod was inspired by Wallerstein, she argued against his idea that the world-system arose in the sixteenth century as well as against the implication that the West was always at its center of the system.

The Work In Its Context

Janet Abu-Lughod's *Before European Hegemony* does not fit neatly into a particular school of thought or academic field. Most major research libraries classify it under medieval economic history, international trade history, medieval cities and towns, and sometimes medieval world history.* Its impact on medieval history and trade history has nevertheless been limited. The book's publisher, Oxford University Press, advertises it as a work of comparative and historical sociology. In university classrooms, where it is widely regarded as a useful teaching text, it appears most frequently on reading lists for courses on world history. In scholarship, its influence has been greatest in research on world-systems, which libraries often classify under social systems or globalization.

> ❝ The world economy of the thirteenth century is not only fascinating in itself but, because it contained no single hegemonic* power, provides an important contrast to the world system that grew out of it: the one Europe reshaped to its own ends and dominated for so long. ❞
>
> Janet Abu-Lughod, *Before European Hegemony: The World-System A.D. 1250–1350*

The strong focus on major cities in *Before European Hegemony* has also stimulated interest in world cities* in the context of world-systems. Taking into account the areas in which Abu-Lughod's book has been most influential, it is perhaps best characterized as a work of world history and world-systems research, with a strong focus on major cities.

When *Before European Hegemony* first appeared in 1989, the most important concerns of world history and world-systems research included the rise of the West after about 1500 and the structure of world-systems. The historical sociologist Immanuel Wallerstein addressed both of these concerns in the first two volumes of his work *The Modern World-System*,[1] which profoundly influenced Abu-Lughod and provided her with an intellectual framework for her research.

Wallerstein's previous studies on Africa led him to recognize that the conventional tools of empirical research (that is, research founded on evidence verifiable by observation) limited the understanding of contemporary realities. He stressed the importance of history while discarding the presumption of modern social science that social boundaries coincided with state boundaries (that is, the presumption that "a people" and "a nation" always share the same interests, identity, and influence). He focused instead on world-systems as the most fitting units for studying social processes. He drew on the work of the Hungarian economic historian Karl Polanyi* and the Austrian economic theorist Joseph Schumpeter,* among others, and borrowed from dependency theory*—a theory that describes the process by which developed "core" countries draw resources from lesser-developed countries—to emphasize the relationship between the world-systems core and peripheral societies beyond the core.[2]

Overview of the Field

Although Abu-Lughod began to draw up her research agenda for *Before European Hegemony* in 1984, her earlier work on Cairo was critical. Her interest in the international trade network of the thirteenth and fourteenth centuries began to take shape in the late 1960s and continued to develop through the 1970s and early 1980s. This was a period during which the *Annales* school of history flourished in France under the leadership of the historian Fernand Braudel,* an advocate of "total history" (*l'histoire totale*), an approach to research and analysis that stressed the comprehensive study of historical issues. Whereas conventional history focused on short-term factors that highlighted events and individuals (*l'histoire événementielle*), historians of the *Annales* school focused on the long term (*longue durée*) and emphasized both geographic and environmental factors and large-scale social and economic structures. This approach to the study of history necessarily drew on the aims and methods of different academic disciplines.

Abu-Lughod embraced an understanding of learning that emphasized its relative character. She drew on the work of physicist and historian of science Thomas Kuhn* (1922–96) to explain the nature of progress in scholarship. Kuhn argued that advances in scholarship do not proceed in a straight line, but result from revolutions or "paradigm shifts" that arise from the build-up of anomalies—that is, pieces of information that diverge from existing models or theories. This eventually leads to a new paradigm, or model, that replaces the old one and opens up new dimensions of understanding.[3] However, whereas Kuhn emphasized anomalies born out of empirical, or factual, observation, Abu-Lughod recognized that anomalies might arise from what the observer brings to bear on the observation, or from the way the observer sees what is being observed.

For Abu-Lughod, the accumulation of anomalies that led to her writing *Before European Hegemony* depended on looking at existing information from a fresh perspective.

Academic Influences

It is difficult to imagine Abu-Lughod's *Before European Hegemony* being written without the influence of the first two volumes of Immanuel Wallerstein's *The Modern World-System*.[4]

Wallerstein's work, the first volumes of which appeared while Abu-Lughod's ideas on the pre-modern world-system were starting to take shape, served as a catalyst for her, speeding things up while providing an intellectual framework for her to develop her ideas around. Abu-Lughod also drew inspiration from Lewis Mumford* (1895–1990), a multidisciplinary scholar who wrote on cities and urbanization, among other things, and won the US National Book Award in 1962 for *The City in History*.[5] Abu-Lughod's deep interest in cities derived largely from her early reading of two of Mumford's works: *Technics and Civilization* and *The Culture of Cities*.[6] These books encouraged her to consider the international trade network of the Middle Ages through the prism of key cities.

Abu-Lughod also identified a gap in the literature. Her readings on the history of individual cities in Europe, the Middle East, and Asia during the Middle Ages led her to search for studies on the links between major cities across the regions. Unable to find any such research, and encouraged by Wallerstein's publication of the first two volumes of his work, she decided to write about the issue herself. *Before European Hegemony*, then, grew out of Abu-Lughod's interest in the kind of large-scale social and economic structures of history described by the *Annales* historians, and the desire to account for the number of historical anomalies that she discovered while looking at history from this fresh perspective. Abu-Lughod also sought to dispel the impression that Wallerstein's modern world-system, taking shape around 1500, was the first of its kind and that the hierarchical structure of Wallerstein's system, in which Europe was dominant, was the only possible structure.

NOTES

1 Immanuel M. Wallerstein, *Capitalist Agriculture and the Origins of the European World-Economy in the Sixteenth Century*, vol. 1 of *The Modern World-System* (New York: Academic Press, 1974); Immanuel M. Wallerstein, *Mercantilism and the Consolidation of the European World-Economy, 1600–1750*, vol. 2 of *The Modern World-System* (New York: Academic Press, 1980).

2 For Wallerstein's own account of his intellectual development, see the "Intellectual Itinerary" page on his website: http://iwallerstein.com/intellectual-itinerary/.

3 Thomas S. Kuhn, *The Structure of Scientific Revolutions* (Chicago: University of Chicago Press, 1961), 52–65.

4 Wallerstein, *Capitalist Agriculture*; Wallerstein, *Mercantilism*.

5 Lewis Mumford, *The City in History: Its Origins, Its Transformations and Its Prospects* (London: Secker & Warburg, 1961); Janet L. Abu-Lughod, "Lewis Mumford's Contributions to the History of Cities: A Critical Appraisal" (paper presented at the first annual Lewis Mumford Lecture, University of Albany, April12, 2000).

6 Lewis Mumford, *Technics and Civilisation* (London: Routledge and Kegan Paul, 1934); Lewis Mumford, *The Culture of Cities* (London: Secker & Warburg, 1938).

MODULE 3
THE PROBLEM

KEY POINTS

- By focusing on the role of the major cities in the international trade network of the thirteenth century, Abu-Lughod showed that a medieval world-system* with three interdependent sub-systems already existed three centuries before the rise of the modern world-system dominated by Europe.

- Abu-Lughod used the same methods that Immanuel Wallerstein* used in his study of *The Modern World-System*—a multidisciplinary, broad geographical approach, paying attention to the views of marginalized people—but with a focus on the medieval world-system.

- *Before European Hegemony* drew together scholarship on cities, cross-cultural exchange, and capitalism* in new ways, showing that the previous views on world-systems, championed by Wallenstein, were incomplete.

Core Question

The core questions that Janet Abu-Lughod sets out to answer in *Before European Hegemony: The World-System A.D. 1250–1350* are long-standing ones—where are we, how did we get here, and where are we going? More specifically, Abu-Lughod seeks to understand the medieval origins of the European-dominated world-system that Immanuel Wallerstein began to describe in the first two volumes of his work *The Modern World-System*, published in 1974 and 1980. The questions she asked concerned what had given rise to the modern system and what that might suggest about its future evolution. Her main task was to describe the world-system that emerged in the

> ❝ In the sixteenth century, Europe took the lead in forging what Wallerstein has termed the 'modern world-system.' In *that* world-system, which has persisted for some 500 years, the West was clearly hegemonic.* But to understand its roots, it is necessary to examine the period *before* European hegemony. ❞
>
> Janet Abu-Lughod, *Before European Hegemony: The World-System A.D. 1250–1350*

thirteenth century, that broke down in the fourteenth century, and that then evolved into the modern system.

Abu-Lughod's questions also grew out of a trend for scholars to approach historical problems in broad geographic, even global, terms (although her questions started to take shape, albeit vaguely, before this trend began). She was responding to the Belgian historian Henri Pirenne's* work on the revival of cities in Europe during the Middle Ages,[1] the German sociologist Max Weber's* sharp distinction between Western and Eastern cities,[2] and the work of Weber and the influential German economist and social theorist Karl Marx* on the origins of capitalism.[3]

Abu-Lughod addressed her core questions by describing in detail the thirteenth-century world-system that predated Wallerstein's modern system and by focusing on the role of major cities in it. The earlier system, she found, was nearly as extensive as the modern one initially was, stretching from Western Europe across the Middle East to East Asia, and was characterized by a comparable level of technological development. It was also made up of roughly the same proportions of free, semi-free, and slave labor, but whereas Europe dominated the modern system, the thirteenth-century system was multi-centered. Europe was merely one of three centers in the medieval system—and arguably not even the most important one.

The Participants

In the first two volumes of *The Modern World-System*, Wallerstein treated the system that emerged around the beginning of the sixteenth century as if it were the first world-system; he agreed that "world empires" had previously existed, but not world-systems in the way that he understood them. A single core in Western Europe dominated the system that Wallerstein began to describe in those volumes. For him, the modern world-system was wholly new; nothing like it had existed before. Wallerstein's work and the scholarly reception of it also tended to fuse together the concept of a world-system and "the particular hierarchical structure of organization" that he described for the modern system, dominated by one region. Wallerstein and other scholars also seemed to exclude the possibility of different organizational structures.[4]

Abu-Lughod regarded some of the ideas behind Wallerstein's modern world-system with suspicion. The modern system must have evolved from an earlier system, she supposed, one that might have been structured differently. This led her to conceive the plan that brought together her ideas on urban development, the role of cities in the world economy, parallel developments in commerce and culture in different parts of the world in the thirteenth century, and evidence for capitalist—or pre-capitalist—behavior before the sixteenth century, not only in Europe but also in the Middle East and Asia. She adopted some of the same methodologies that Wallerstein used. She took account of subaltern* perspectives (that is, the views of people from outside the power structure as opposed to the views from the upper levels of the power structure), and used a multidisciplinary approach and a broad geographical scope. Among her influences were scholars of world history* such as William McNeill* and French historians of the *Annales* school,* especially Fernand Braudel.*

The Contemporary Debate

By the time *Before European Hegemony* first appeared, other scholars had already raised the question of whether the modern world-system that Wallerstein described was the first such system.[5] In the years preceding its publication, too, other authors had examined cross-cultural exchange and the development of social power across even broader ranges of time and space.[6] With her book, however, Abu-Lughod put forward the strongest case yet for pushing the study of world-systems back before 1500 and encouraged other scholars to use the methodological and theoretical framework of world-systems analysis to consider even earlier periods.[7] Abu-Lughod concluded that Wallerstein's modern world-system was evolving towards a more multi-centered system in which Asia will play a more decisive role. This has encouraged other scholars to investigate the question of Asia's growing importance in the world more deeply.[8]

Before European Hegemony must be seen as a direct response to Wallerstein's description of the modern world-system. Abu-Lughod drew attention to the shortcomings of Wallerstein's vision. She further developed it by pushing the analysis back to the thirteenth century and describing a medieval world-system that was very different in structure from the system that followed it. Abu-Lughod also took the opportunity to focus on the role of key cities in the medieval system while dealing with perennial questions about the revival of cities in the Middle Ages, distinctions between Eastern and Western cities, and the origins of capitalism. In this way, *Before European Hegemony* ties together, extends, and modifies several different lines of scholarship on cities, cross-cultural exchange, and capitalism in novel ways. The core ideas that Abu-Lughod expresses in her book are not so different from those of other authors; what is especially novel, is the way that she deals with them, by treating them together on a vast scale.

NOTES

1   Henri Pirenne, *Medieval Cities: Their Origins and the Revival of Trade*, trans. Frank D. Halsey (Princeton, NJ: Princeton University Press, 1925); Henri Pirenne, *Mohammed and Charlemagne*, trans. Bernard Miall (London: Allen & Unwin, 1939).

2   Max Weber, *The City*, trans. Don Martindale and Gertrud Neuwirth (Glencoe, IL: Free Press, 1958).

3   Karl Marx, *Pre-Capitalist Economic Formations*, trans. Jack Cohen, ed. Eric Hobsbawm (London: Lawrence & Wishart, 1964); Max Weber, *The Protestant Ethic and the Spirit of Capitalism*, trans. Talcott Parsons (London: Allen & Unwin, 1930).

4   Janet L. Abu-Lughod, *Before European Hegemony: The World-System A.D. 1250–1350* (Oxford: Oxford University Press, 1989), 38, n. 2.

5   See Jane Schneider, "Was There a pre-Capitalist World-System?" *Peasant Studies* 6 (1977): 20–7; Kajsa Ekholm and Jonathan Friedman, "Capitalism, Imperialism and Exploitation in the Ancient World-Systems," *Review* 6 (1982): 87–110.

6   See Philip D. Curtin, *Cross-Cultural Exchange in World History* (Cambridge: Cambridge University Press, 1984); Michael Mann, *A History of Power from the Beginning to AD 1760*, vol. 1 of *The Sources of Social Power* (Cambridge: Cambridge University Press, 1986).

7   See Thomas D. Hall and Christopher Chase-Dunn, "Forward into the Past: World-Systems before 1500," *Sociological Forum* 9 (1994): 295–306.

8   Andre Gunder Frank, *ReOrient: Global Economy in the Asian Age* (Berkeley: University of California Press, 1998).

MODULE 4
THE AUTHOR'S CONTRIBUTION

KEY POINTS

- Abu-Lughod's work was highly innovative, showing that already in the thirteenth century there existed a world-system* in which Europe, the Middle East, and Asia interacted on equal terms through a network of "world cities."*

- *Before European Hegemony* focuses on how interactions between world cities across Eurasia not only created a global network but also influenced economies in hinterlands,* or rural areas around cities.

- Abu-Lughod's conception of the medieval world-system was built on Immanuel Wallerstein's* pioneering study of the modern world-system, her own long-term interest in cities, and the growing interest in multidisciplinary research.

Author's Aims

Before European Hegemony: The World-System A.D. 1250–1350 grew out of Janet Abu-Lughod's deep interest in the history of individual cities across Europe, the Middle East, and Asia during the Middle Ages. This led her to seek out studies that focused on major cities and the connections between them in the period around the year 1300, which she viewed as a time of economic and cultural development. Unable to find such a study and inspired by the publication of the first two volumes of Immanuel Wallerstein's* *The Modern World-System*,[1] she set out herself to write a book that provided the answers. For Wallerstein, the modern world–system was the first of its kind when it emerged in the sixteenth century; it was also hierarchical, with a single dominant core in Europe that later also extended across the Atlantic Ocean to include North America. Abu-Lughod disagreed both with Wallerstein's

> **❝** All of these units [across Europe, the Middle East, and Asia] were not only trading with one another and handling the transit trade of others, but had begun to reorganize parts of their internal economies to meet the exigencies of the world market. **❞**
>
> Janet Abu-Lughod, *Before European Hegemony: The World-System A.D. 1250–1350*

description of the modern system as the first such system and with the claim that world-systems were always hierarchical. Wallerstein's work nevertheless provided Abu-Lughod with the conceptual framework around which to write the book that she wanted to read.

The result was *Before European Hegemony*, which proved to be a highly original work that challenged the ideas held by many scholars. Abu-Lughod's study of the medieval world-system pushed the emerging field of world-systems analysis back to the decades around the year 1300, when she believed the world had achieved an unprecedented degree of "economic integration and cultural efflorescence [or flowering]."[2] It also raised questions about the structure of world-systems, suggesting that the organization of Wallerstein's modern system with its single core was not the only possible form of organization. What was most unique about Abu-Lughod's exploration of the medieval world-system was its constant emphasis on the role of key cities as crucial links in the international trade network.

Approach

Two of the main questions that Janet Abu-Lughod posed in *Before European Hegemony* grew directly out of Immanuel Wallerstein's description of the modern world-system. She asked, first of all, what came before Wallerstein's modern system, and second, what the structure of the system that preceded the modern one had been.

Through her extensive readings, Abu-Lughod was aware of ties between cities in the Middle Ages that had sometimes stretched, whether directly or indirectly, over vast distances. From her previous work on Cairo,[3] she also realized that Europe and the West had not always been as politically and economically dominant as they became from the sixteenth century onwards.

Influenced by Wallerstein's analysis of the modern world-system, she began to see interactions between distant cities before the middle of the fourteenth century in terms of a medieval world-system. Unlike Wallerstein's modern system, however, the medieval system that Abu-Lughod identified was a multi-centered system in which no single region was dominant over the others. In this way she challenged both Wallerstein's claim that the modern world-system was the first of its kind and the implication that world-systems were always hierarchical.

While rejecting Wallerstein's hierarchical conception of world-systems, *Before European Hegemony* brought together several different strands of Abu-Lughod's thought. Perhaps the most original and stimulating aspects of the book derive from her view of the medieval world-system as an "archipelago of towns" or "world cities,"*[4] which underscores the uneven nature of development within the system. The world cities that enabled interactions between different parts of the overall system stood out sharply from the rest, towering far above the rural isolation that characterized most of the system. Abu-Lughod focused on major cities not simply because they were high points in the system, but also because the interrelationships between them, whether direct or indirect, strongly influenced the organization of production and labor in and around them and "defined the contours of the larger system."[5]

Contribution in Context

Abu-Lughod's *Before European Hegemony* presents various ideas that were current when she was writing. Wallerstein's analysis of the modern world-system was vital because it provided Abu-Lughod with the intellectual framework for her study of the medieval world-system. Her reflections on the influential American science historian Thomas Kuhn's* theory of scientific progress were also important because they led her to consider the benefits of looking at existing information in new ways. She sought to achieve a fresh perspective on the existing data by embracing a cross-disciplinary approach, taking greater account of subaltern* interpretations, and adopting a global outlook, all of which represented popular trends in scholarship when she was writing.

Finally, Abu-Lughod further developed her own deep interest in cities by examining the medieval world-system through the prism of key cities.

It is difficult to imagine that Abu-Lughod would have ever written her book on the world-system of the thirteenth and fourteenth centuries had the first two volumes of Wallerstein's work on the modern system not existed. It must be stressed, however, that *Before European Hegemony* was wholly new. No one had ever before sought to describe the entire medieval world-system of Europe, the Middle East, and Asia. Scholars had generally considered the three main regions separately; at best, they sometimes studied interactions between two of the three regions, but not all of them, and certainly not on equal terms. Even today, Abu-Lughod's analysis of the medieval world-system remains the most comprehensive investigation of the subject.

The book was also original in the extent to which it considered existing information in new ways. In her description of the medieval world-system, Abu-Lughod crossed disciplinary lines, drawing on many different academic disciplines; she also balanced dominant Western and subaltern perspectives, and took a global view specifically to study "connections between geographic entities that are usually treated by different sets of specialists."[6] The originality of the project lay partly in the blending of these elements and, most importantly, in its focus on key cities.

NOTES

1   Immanuel M. Wallerstein, *Capitalist Agriculture and the Origins of the European World-Economy in the Sixteenth Century*, vol. 1 of *The Modern World-System* (New York: Academic Press, 1974); Immanuel M. Wallerstein, *Mercantilism and the Consolidation of the European World-Economy, 1600–1750*, vol. 2 of *The Modern World-System* (New York: Academic Press, 1980).

2   Janet L. Abu-Lughod, *Before European Hegemony: The World-System A.D. 1250–1350* (Oxford: Oxford University Press, 1989), 4.

3   Janet L. Abu-Lughod, *Cairo: 1001 Years of the City Victorious* (Princeton, NJ: Princeton University Press, 1971).

4   Abu-Lughod, *Before European Hegemony*, 13–14, 269, 348, 353.

5   Abu-Lughod, *Before European Hegemony*, 32–3.

6   Abu-Lughod, *Before European Hegemony*, ix.

SECTION 2
IDEAS

MODULE 5
MAIN IDEAS

KEY POINTS

- *Before European Hegemony* suggests that advances in various spheres, especially navigation and statecraft, helped create the new international trade network that took shape across Europe, the Middle East, and Asia during the thirteenth century.

- Abu-Lughod argues that the West's rise to domination of the world-system* in the sixteenth century was not because of its strength but rather because of a failure of the East, due to the catastrophic effects of the fourteenth-century Black Death* alongside the collapse of the Mongol Peace.*

- Although Abu-Lughod did not contribute new terminology, she helped to spread concepts proposed by other scholars, such as "archipelago of towns" and "world cities."*

Key Themes

In *Before European Hegemony: The World-System A.D. 1250–1350*, Janet Abu-Lughod deals with a range of themes, of which two stand out.

The book's first main theme is that increased economic integration and cultural development in Europe, the Middle East, and Asia in the thirteenth century signaled the rise of a new international trade network that amounted to a world-system.[1] European economic expansion was crucial to the development of this new world-system. An extensive trading system between the Middle East and China was already in place when Europe "reached out" in the twelfth and thirteenth centuries to join it, creating a broader world-system.[2] The new system was marked by parallel developments in a variety of

> **❝** By the eleventh and, even more, twelfth century, many parts of the Old World began to become integrated into a system of exchange ... The apogee of this cycle came between the end of the thirteenth and the first decades of the fourteenth century, by which time even Europe and China had established direct, if decidedly limited, contact with each other. **❞**
>
> Janet Abu-Lughod, *Before European Hegemony: The World-System A.D. 1250–1350*

spheres, including navigation and statecraft, which made communication and exchange easier. These developments transformed large parts of the world from a mosaic of essentially isolated economies into an international trade network that Abu-Lughod describes as a medieval world–system.

The second main theme of *Before European Hegemony* is that development in the system was uneven. Much of the system remained mainly agricultural, subsistence oriented (supplying little more than the immediate needs of the local population), and isolated. The points of contact in the system were merchant communities situated mostly in major cities and towns. Some of these places were strictly trading enclaves without hinterlands,* but most were able to draw on resources and production in these rural areas surrounding them. The interactions between these cities and towns with other parts of the system shaped production and the organization of labor in the surrounding hinterlands to enable export to take place. Abu Lughod likens these points of contact to islands that stood above "a vast sea of encapsulated rural regions."[3] She describes the system as an "archipelago of towns" or "world cities" to stress this fundamental feature of the system. Her study of the medieval world–system focuses on these high points.

Exploring The Ideas

In her introduction, Abu-Lughod frames the main idea of *Before European Hegemony* in terms of what she calls the descriptive task. She sets out to describe the international trade network in the thirteenth and fourteenth centuries, when Eurasia achieved unprecedented "economic integration and cultural efflorescence [blossoming]."[4] She describes in turn the European, Middle Eastern, and Asian parts of this network, dedicating equal space to each of these three main sub-systems, and argues that the connections between them amount to a world-system. She devotes most of her book to this descriptive task, focusing on the major cities in the medieval world-system that facilitated interaction.

Abu-Lughod's description of the medieval world-system demonstrates that Immanuel Wallerstein's* modern system,[5] which began to emerge around the year 1500, evolved from an earlier system. Whereas the structure of Wallerstein's modern system was hierarchical, the earlier system was egalitarian, characterized by equality. This shows that world-systems change over time and raises questions about the transition from the medieval system to the modern one and the rapid rise of the West in the modern system.

Abu-Lughod addresses these questions only very briefly, which is perhaps surprising given her claim that the rise of the West in the modern system was not based on any "inherent historical necessity" or "unique entrepreneurial spirit."[6] She argues instead that the rise of the West depended on the fall of the East. The Black Death, a widespread outbreak of plague across Europe and Asia in the fourteenth century, devastated the entire system. The collapse of the Mongol Peace, or *Pax Mongolica*—the relative peace that held across most of the Eurasian land mass under the huge empire founded by the Mongol* leader Genghis Khan—and the breakdown of the Asian trade network nevertheless affected only the East. Consequently, the West was able to adapt more easily to the new conditions and dictate the terms of trade in its relations with the East.

Language And Expression

Abu-Lughod's account is clear and economical. Her prose is fluid, almost conversational, and largely free of jargon, even if her arguments are often complex, nuanced, and occasionally combative. On occasion she puts forward arguments that are poorly supported by the evidence and fails to recognize the uncertainties that surround some of the written histories she cites. On the whole, however, Abu-Lughod expresses her ideas in a manner that promotes rather than hinders understanding and that therefore broadens the book's appeal.

In effect, *Before European Hegemony* is written on two levels. Its arguments are clear to advanced undergraduate and graduate students, it engages in long-standing debates, and it encourages classroom discussion; this has helped to make the book a valuable teaching text. At the same time, it is an intellectually challenging work that raises new questions of interest to avant-garde scholars about the nature and structure of world-systems. It also stresses the importance of giving equal weight to dominant and subaltern* perspectives, while breaking down barriers that usually separate distinct geographical regions of scholarly research.

Because Abu-Lughod wrote in a simple and straightforward language and style, she did relatively little to enrich the academic vocabulary. Instead, she promoted phrases coined by others. Fernand Braudel,* the leader of the *Annales* school of history,* had borrowed the expression "archipelago of towns" from the German historian Rudolf Häpke, and used it to describe the unevenness of development in the early modern period.[7] Abu-Lughod saw this as "a particularly sensitive way to capture the fact that, within the same general region, a variety of social formations co-existed."[8] For her, the medieval world-system consisted of a relatively small number of commercially oriented urban centers that stood above vast areas of rural isolation in which production was overwhelmingly agrarian and subsistence oriented. The trading centers were the points of contact that facilitated interaction between different parts of the overall system and "defined the contours of the larger system."[9]

Borrowing another expression, Abu-Lughod described these places as "world cities."[10] Both of these concepts have entered the academic vocabulary, though perhaps more so in the case of the latter, around which a body of literature emerged during the 1990s.[11]

NOTES

1   Janet L. Abu-Lughod, *Before European Hegemony: The World-System A.D. 1250–1350* (Oxford: Oxford University Press, 1989), 4.

2   Abu-Lughod, *Before European Hegemony*, 12.

3   Abu-Lughod, *Before European Hegemony*, 14.

4   Abu-Lughod, *Before European Hegemony*, 4.

5   Immanuel M. Wallerstein, *Capitalist Agriculture and the Origins of the European World-Economy in the Sixteenth Century*, vol. 1 of *The Modern World-System* (New York: Academic Press, 1974); Immanuel M. Wallerstein, *Mercantilism and the Consolidation of the European World-Economy, 1600–1750*, vol. 2 of *The Modern World-System* (New York: Academic Press, 1980).

6   Abu-Lughod, *Before European Hegemony*, 12, 18, 361.

7   Fernand Braudel, *The Perspective of the World*, vol. 3 of *Capitalism and Civilization, 15th–18th Century*, trans. Sian Reynolds (London: William Collins, 1984), 30.

8   Abu-Lughod, *Before European Hegemony*, 13.

9   Abu-Lughod, *Before European Hegemony*, 33.

10 John Friedmann and Goetz Wolff, "World City Formation: An Agenda for Research and Action," *International Journal of Urban and Regional Research* 6 (1982): 309–43.

11 Saskia Sassen, *Cities in a World Economy* (Thousand Oaks, CA: Pine Forge Press, 1994); Andrew Bosworth, "World Cities and World Economic Cycles," in *Civilisations and World Systems: Studying World-Historical Change*, ed. Stephen K. Sanderson (Walnut Creek, CA: Altamira Press, 1995), 206–27; Peter L. Knox and Peter J. Taylor, eds, *World Cities in a World-System* (Cambridge: Cambridge University Press, 1995); Janet L. Abu-Lughod, "Comparing Chicago, New York, and Los Angeles: Testing Some World-Cities Hypotheses," in *World-Cities in a World-System*, ed. Peter L. Knox and Peter J. Taylor (Cambridge: Cambridge University Press, 1995), 171–91; Janet L. Abu-Lughod, *New York, Chicago, Los Angeles: America's Global Cities* (Minneapolis: University of Minnesota Press, 1999).

SECONDARY IDEAS

KEY POINTS

- The secondary themes of *Before European Hegemony* are that the medieval world-system* took shape when Europe joined a preexisting Middle Eastern and Asian trading network; that economies in the system were pre-capitalist, not capitalist;* and that world-systems are constantly evolving.

- Abu-Lughod claimed that Europe was the least developed of the three main regions. However, after the fourteenth-century plague and the instability that emerged in the East with the collapse of the Mongol* Empire, Europe began to emerge as the dominant part of the system.

- Although not well developed in her book and therefore of limited impact, Abu-Lughod's ideas about the origins of the medieval world-system and the transition from the medieval to the modern system offer the greatest scope for future research.

Other Ideas

Some of the more important secondary ideas of Janet Abu-Lughod's *Before European Hegemony* are that Europe was initially a peripheral part of the medieval world-system; that the economies in the system were pre-capitalist rather than capitalist; that world-systems evolve constantly; and that the rise of the West in the modern system depended on the failure of the East in the medieval system. When Europe began to emerge as a participant in the system during the twelfth century, the Middle East and Asia already formed an extensive trading network that stretched from the Mediterranean to China. The rise of the medieval

> ❝ Before Europe became *one* of the world-economies in the twelfth and thirteenth centuries, when it joined the long-distance trade system that stretched through the Mediterranean into the Red Sea and Persian Gulf and on into the Indian Ocean and through the strait of Malacca to reach China, there were numerous pre-existent world-economies. ❞
>
> Janet Abu-Lughod, *Before European Hegemony: The World-System A.D. 1250–1350*

world-system occurred when Europe "reached out" to join this "ongoing operation."[1] By 1300, some of the more advanced economies in the world-system appeared to possess capitalistic features. However, because of wide variations within the system and the continued existence of feudal* forms of social organization (based on who worked land and who claimed supreme authority by owning it), Abu-Lughod characterized the overall economy as pre-capitalist rather than capitalist.[2]

The historical sociologist Immanuel Wallerstein's* description of the world-system in his multi-volume work *The Modern World-System*[3] was of a static entity; Abu-Lughod, on the other hand, emphasized the way that world-systems are always evolving. The modern system, she argued, had arisen from the ruins of an earlier one that flourished in the thirteenth and fourteenth centuries; the medieval system, in turn, had evolved from an even earlier one in Roman antiquity. The dominant position of the West in the modern world-system hinged upon the more complete disintegration of the East in the medieval system.

Exploring The Ideas

Among Abu-Lughod's most important secondary ideas are those concerning the transition from the more balanced medieval world-system to Wallerstein's European-dominated modern system. Whereas Wallerstein's modern system was hierarchical, with the core in Western Europe exercising hegemony*—that is, dominance—over the semi-peripheral and peripheral areas, Abu-Lughod's medieval system included no distinct core that dominated the rest of the system. Before the middle of the fourteenth century, Europe, the Middle East, and Asia interacted on fairly equal terms, though Europe was the least advanced member, China was "the leading contender for hegemony," and "the Middle East was generally more developed than Europe."[4] The transition from the medieval system to the modern system, then, raises questions about the nature and structure of world-systems and the rapid rise of the West in the modern system.

According to Abu-Lughod, world-systems are constantly evolving. They emerge, flourish, collapse, reconstitute into new systems, and thrive again. At any given point, the world-system "is in the throes of change."[5] The high point of the medieval system around 1300 was simply a phase in the continuous evolution and restructuring of the world-system. This makes it difficult to determine the precise point at which Wallerstein's modern system rose from the wreckage of the medieval system and when the egalitarian structure of the medieval system gave way to the hierarchical structure of the modern one. Abu-Lughod argues that the West owes its dominant position in the modern system to its more successful adaptation to the changing circumstances after the Black Death.* Although the Black Death affected the entire system, the collapse of the so-called *Pax Mongolica* (Mongol Peace)* in the East worsened the breakdown there. When the East failed to adapt to the new conditions, Europeans took advantage of their stronger position and adopted an approach to inter-regional exchange that Abu-Lughod characterizes as "trade-cum-plunder," based more on short-term gains than on long-term relations.[6]

Overlooked

Most of Abu-Lughod's book focuses on her description of the thirteenth century world-system; it gives relatively little space to its secondary themes. The notion that Europe was overshadowed by the Middle East and Asia before the thirteenth century is not entirely new, but has more commonly been discussed in the context of research on either the Middle East or Asia, as in the French historian Maurice Lombard's* classic study of *The Golden Age of Islam* (1975), which Abu-Lughod curiously overlooks. In *Before European Hegemony*, she merely broaches the idea that Europe initially stood at the edge of an earlier system but does not develop the theme into any detailed consideration of the beginnings or origins of the medieval world-system. Research since the book's publication has sometimes touched upon the question of Europe's relations with the Middle East and Asia before 1200—but never in a balanced and complete manner that devotes equal space to all regions and takes adequate account of the different points of view involved.

The origins of capitalism, as a focus of academic research, remain a subject of spirited classroom discussion and continue to generate a sizable body of literature. There is no suggestion, however, that Abu-Lughod's book contributed significantly to the debate. Her claim that world-systems are in a constant state of change yielded little resistance, which suggests that scholars generally accepted the idea. Immanuel Wallerstein wholly agreed with Abu-Lughod's conclusions in this regard.[7] Nevertheless, the German American economic historian Andre Gunder Frank* believed that she failed to push this point far enough. He argued for placing the medieval world-system within the even wider context of "a single and continuous" world-system over a much longer period.[8] The argument that the rise of the West hinged on the fall of the East has attracted more attention than other secondary themes, but scholars have pursued the question only briefly in book reviews rather than in full studies of the transition from the medieval system to the modern one. Abu-Lughod's contention that it was the Europeans who responded most robustly to the disruptions of the mid-fourteenth century seems to have lacked sufficient detail to encourage further inquiry.

NOTES

1   Janet L. Abu-Lughod, *Before European Hegemony: The World-System A.D. 1250–1350* (Oxford: Oxford University Press, 1989), 6.

2   Abu-Lughod, *Before European Hegemony*, 115–16.

3   Immanuel M. Wallerstein, *Capitalist Agriculture and the Origins of the European World-Economy in the Sixteenth Century*, vol. 1 of *The Modern World-System* (New York: Academic Press, 1974); Immanuel M. Wallerstein, *Mercantilism and the Consolidation of the European World-Economy, 1600– 1750*, vol. 2 of *The Modern World-System* (New York: Academic Press, 1980).

4   Abu-Lughod, *Before European Hegemony*, 14.

5   Abu-Lughod, *Before European Hegemony*, 6.

6   Abu-Lughod, *Before European Hegemony*, 361.

7   Immanuel M. Wallerstein, "Review of Janet Abu-Lughod, *Before European Hegemony*," *International Journal of Middle East Studies* 24 (1992): 131.

8   Andre Gunder Frank, "The Thirteenth-Century World-System: A Review Essay," *Journal of World History* 1 (1990): 254–5.

MODULE 7
ACHIEVEMENT

KEY POINTS

- Abu-Lughod's book describes in detail the interdependent medieval world-system* and briefly considers its decline and transition into the modern system dominated by the West. Her argument that the rise of the West in the modern system was due to the more complete collapse of the East nevertheless lacks depth and is less convincing than other parts of the book.

- Growing interest in world history* and world-systems analysis and the author's broad geographical and multidisciplinary approach both contributed to the popularity of *Before European Hegemony*.

- Since the publication of Abu-Lughod's book, scholars have taken for granted the existence of an earlier world-system more than two centuries before the emergence of the modern world-system.

Assessing The Argument

Janet Abu-Lughod's *Before European Hegemony: The World-System A.D. 1250–1350* focuses on key cities in Europe, the Middle East, and Asia and the connections between them prior to the formation of the modern world-system dominated by Europe. She describes the world-system of the later thirteenth and early fourteenth centuries when, she believes, the world achieved an unprecedented degree of economic integration and cultural development. She dedicates most of her book to this central task and successfully demonstrates that major cities across the three main regions were bound together in an overarching world-system. Although some of

> **❝** What we have is a very convincing exposition of the emergence in this period of a very vast trading network without a clear argument that could enable us to decide whether its emergence was structurally inevitable or merely conjuncturally possible or perhaps just a fluke. **❞**
>
> Immanuel Wallerstein, Review of *Before European Hegemony*

the detail is open to question, the argument, as a sum of its parts, stands up well.

Abu-Lughod also considers how the thirteenth-century world-system was structured, why it was structured in the way that it was, how and why it collapsed, and how it evolved into the modern system described by Immanuel Wallerstein.*[1] She devotes only the introduction and conclusion of her book to these issues, however, and her achievement in these respects was limited. In particular, her argument that the rise of the West beginning in the fifteenth century depended upon the fall of the East lacks depth and rigor. She successfully shows that Wallerstein's modern system arose from the remnants of the medieval system and that the three main regions in the medieval system interacted on fairly equal terms (a proposition that suggests that the hierarchical structure Wallerstein describes in his work is not the only possible structure for world-systems). The interdependent character of the medieval system, in contrast with the European-dominated modern system, also illustrates the changeable nature of world-systems and raises questions about the future evolution of the present system.

Achievement In Context
New trends in scholarship contributed to the success of Janet Abu-Lughod's *Before European Hegemony*. When the book appeared,

world history and world-systems analysis were still relatively young branches of scholarship. *Before European Hegemony* benefited from the rise of world history as a distinct academic discipline and from surging interest in world-systems analysis on the strength of the first two volumes of Wallerstein's multi-volume study *The Modern World-System*, the first two volumes of which were published in 1974 and 1980. Abu-Lughod's multidisciplinary approach also appealed to a growing appetite for cross-disciplinary research. Her book's broad geographic scope further contributed to its success. It was and still is highly unusual for a work of medieval economic history to cover Europe, the Middle East, and Asia on even terms.

Finally, the focus on key cities played an important part in the work's success. Abu-Lughod looked at the international economy of the thirteenth and fourteenth centuries through the prism of key "world cities"* and described the way in which those cities facilitated interaction between different parts of the network.

The degree to which developments in the wider world facilitated the reception of *Before European Hegemony* is unclear. The publication of the book in 1989 coincided with great events, including the civil unrest in China exemplified by the Tiananmen Square* protests, and popular revolutions against communist* regimes in Eastern Europe, which led to the collapse of the Berlin Wall* in 1989, the fall of the communist regimes in Europe, and the end of the Cold War*—a decades-long period of tension between the United States and the Soviet Union* and nations aligned to them. According to one commentator, Abu-Lughod's book reflected the extent to which these events caused "the great nineteenth century paradigms of sociology and Marxism"* to lose their intellectual appeal.[2] Suffice to say that Abu-Lughod began work on *Before European Hegemony* long before these events occurred.

Limitations

Although Janet Abu-Lughod seized an opportunity to break new ground in a relatively young and fashionable branch of scholarship when she wrote *Before European Hegemony*, she devotes most of her book to stating what turned out to be obvious. Perhaps the book's greatest limitation is that its main arguments were quickly accepted. In response to Wallerstein's assertion that the modern world-system was the first such system,[3] Abu-Lughod argued that the modern system had evolved from an earlier system that flourished in around 1300 but that broke down after the middle of the fourteenth century. According to Abu-Lughod, the international trade network of the later thirteenth and early fourteenth centuries that joined together the economies of Europe, the Middle East, and Asia indeed constituted a world-system; Wallerstein readily agreed.[4] Since the publication of *Before European Hegemony*, the existence of world-systems before 1500 has been taken for granted.

Abu-Lughod dedicates such a large share of her book to describing the medieval world-system and proving its existence that she is able to discuss her other claims only very briefly. She notes, for example, that Wallerstein's work and its reception tended to conflate the concept of world-system "with the particular hierarchical structure of organization" that he described for the modern system.[5] This seemed to exclude the possibility of structurally different world-systems, but Abu-Lughod argues that the three main regions in the medieval system interacted relatively equally. Wallerstein and most other commentators accepted her argument in this regard, but reactions to some of her other claims were more divided. In particular, her argument that the "rise of the West" from about 1500 was predicated on the "fall of the East", despite Wallerstein's agreement,[6] was inadequately developed and poorly supported by the evidence.

NOTES

1   Immanuel M. Wallerstein, *Capitalist Agriculture and the Origins of the European World-Economy in the Sixteenth Century*, vol. 1 of *The Modern World-System* (New York: Academic Press, 1974); Immanuel M. Wallerstein, *Mercantilism and the Consolidation of the European World-Economy, 1600–1750*, vol. 2 of *The Modern World-System* (New York: Academic Press, 1980).

2   Albert Bergesen, "Pre vs. Post 1500ers," *Comparative Civilisations Review* 30 (1994): 81–9.

3   Wallerstein, *Capitalist Agriculture*; Wallerstein, *Mercantilism*.

4   Immanuel M. Wallerstein, "Review of Janet Abu-Lughod, *Before European Hegemony*," *International Journal of Middle East Studies* 24 (1992): 129–30.

5   Janet L. Abu-Lughod, *Before European Hegemony: The World-System A.D. 1250–1350* (Oxford: Oxford University Press, 1989), 38, n. 2.

6   Wallerstein, "Review of Abu-Lughod, *Before European Hegemony*."

PLACE IN THE AUTHOR'S WORK

KEY POINTS

- *Before European Hegemony* develops Abu-Lughod's persistent focus on cities, the common denominator in all her work, and takes it in new directions.

- The book represents a turning point in the author's career between her earlier work on cities in the developing world and her later work, which focused on the three largest cities in the United States.

- As soon as it appeared, *Before European Hegemony* won critical praise and became a popular staple on college reading lists.

Positioning

When Janet Abu-Lughod published *Before European Hegemony: The World-System A.D. 1250–1350* in 1989, she was nearly 60 and had spent her entire adult life as an academic. The book is the work of a mature scholar and the culmination of a long and fruitful career. But it also marks a turning point for the author.

Until 1980, Abu-Lughod's work focused on two cities in Egypt and Morocco—Cairo and Rabat, respectively.[1] During the same period, she also co-edited a collection of essays and readings on urbanization in the developing world.[2] In *Before European Hegemony*, Abu-Lughod turns her attention to the new field of world-systems analysis* to describe the international trade network of the Middle Ages and the role of key cities in binding the system together.

Although cities continued to occupy a leading position in Abu-Lughod's research after the book's publication, she largely turned

> ❝ The new emphasis on the thirteenth century, the focus on urban formations, and the insistence on the need to differentiate among principles of world system organization [represent] a particularly helpful extension of our historical horizons and a recognition that past and present are not easily collapsed into a single conceptual framework. ❞
>
> Donald Nielsen, "After World Systems Theory"

away from the study of the medieval world-system. Her subsequent published output on the medieval world-system and on world-systems more generally was limited largely to evaluations of world-systems analysis in the years that immediately followed the appearance of *Before European Hegemony*.[3] In later work, Abu-Lughod focused on urban history and sociology, with specific interest in New York, Chicago, and Los Angeles.[4] This was an extension of her interest in world-systems, at least insofar as her studies of these "world cities"* take account of the global context, but they also mark a turning away from the pre-modern world-systems.

Integration

Janet Abu-Lughod's career and published output followed a well-defined path. Her early work on Cairo led her to recognize the inadequacy of conventional histories of the Middle Ages written from Western perspectives. As she read extensively on the histories of individual cities in Europe, the Middle East, and Asia, she became aware of connections and parallel patterns of development between the different regions. This encouraged her to search for books that would explain these connections and parallels.

In 1974, as Abu-Lughod was developing this project, Immanuel Wallerstein* published the first volume of his multi-volume study, *The Modern World-System*.[5] Although still not exactly the book that Abu-Lughod wanted to read, she at least found in it an intellectual framework around which to build her own description of the medieval world-system. This led her, in 1984, to begin to devise a plan for writing the book that she really wanted to read—which turned out to be, five years later, *Before European Hegemony*.

Crucially, Abu-Lughod's deep interest in cities and urban development led her to pursue her study of the medieval world-system through the prism of "world cities"—places, that is, through which different parts of the system interact. After the publication of *Before European Hegemony*, she devoted relatively little attention to the medieval world-system but continued to study world cities, focusing on the three largest cities in the United States. Abu-Lughod's body of work may therefore be seen in terms of two distinct halves, with cities and urban development occupying prominent places in both. The first, lasting until about 1980, focused on cities in the developing world, above all in North Africa; the second, from about 1990, focused on global cities in the United States. *Before European Hegemony* forms the hinge between the two parts.

Significance

Before European Hegemony stands out as Janet Abu-Lughod's most important scholarly achievement because of its multidisciplinary approach, geographic breadth, and theoretical framework. It is also the most historical of her works. Its publication came at the time of— and contributed to—the rise of world-systems analysis and world history* as distinct fields of study. The book generated great interest across several disciplines and almost immediately began to appear on advanced undergraduate and graduate reading lists. It has been particularly successful as a teaching text and continues to be used widely in teaching today.

Abu-Lughod's other major works, both before and after *Before European Hegemony*, have all enjoyed critical success. Her 1971 work on Cairo established her reputation and has more recently won recognition as an American Council of Learned Societies (ACLS) Humanities E-Book.[6] The collection of essays and readings on urbanization in the developing world that Abu-Lughod co-edited in 1977 continues to appear on university reading lists.[7] Her later studies on the largest cities in the United States likewise won critical acclaim when they were published.[8] Abu-Lughod's contributions to scholarship earned her a series of respected fellowships and awards, including a Guggenheim Fellowship in 1976 (for the 1977–78 academic year) and a Distinguished Career Award from the American Sociological Association in its Political Economy of the World System section in 1999.[9] *Before European Hegemony*, however, has attracted more attention from a broader audience than any of her other books.

In effect, *Before European Hegemony* took Abu-Lughod to a new level. Whereas her earlier works were narrowly focused historical studies of urban societies in the Middle East and North Africa, *Before European Hegemony* not only turned her into a scholar of world-systems and world cities but also gained her recognition among medieval and economic historians. Significantly, as the constant feature of her research has been the city, she decided to conduct this study of the international trade network that linked Europe, the Middle East, and Asia in the thirteenth and fourteenth centuries through the prism of key cities in the system. In her later works, she focused on the more recent histories of the three largest cities in the United States. Despite the varied character of Abu-Lughod's scholarship, she has focused on cities throughout the course of her career.

NOTES

1   Janet L. Abu-Lughod, *Cairo: 1001 Years of the City Victorious* (Princeton, NJ: Princeton University Press, 1971; available as ACLS Humanities E-Book at http://www.humanitiesebook.org/); Janet L. Abu-Lughod, *Rabat: Urban Apartheid in Morocco* (Princeton, NJ: Princeton University Press, 1980).

2   Janet L. Abu-Lughod and Richard A. Hay, eds, *Third World Urbanization* (Chicago: Maaroufa Press, 1977).

3   Janet L. Abu-Lughod, "Restructuring the Premodern World-System," *Review* 13 (1990): 273–86; Janet L. Abu-Lughod, "Reply to Donald Nielsen's 'After World Systems Theory'," *International Journal of Politics, Culture and Society* 4 (1991): 499–500; Janet L. Abu-Lughod, "Going Beyond Global Babble," in *Culture, Globalisation and the World-System: Contemporary Conditions for the Representations of Identity*, ed. Anthony D. King (Basingstoke: Macmillan, 1991),131–7; Janet L. Abu-Lughod, "The World System Perspective in the Construction of Economic History," *History and Theory* 34 (1995): 86–98.

4   Janet L. Abu-Lughod, "Comparing Chicago, New York, and Los Angeles: Testing Some World-Cities Hypotheses," in *World-Cities in a World-System*, ed. Peter L. Knox and Peter J. Taylor (Cambridge: Cambridge University Press, 1995), 171–91; Janet L. Abu-Lughod, *New York, Chicago, Los Angeles: America's Global Cities* (Minneapolis: University of Minnesota Press, 1999); Janet L. Abu-Lughod, *Race, Space, and Riots in Chicago, New York, and Los Angeles* (Oxford: Oxford University Press, 2007).

5   Immanuel M. Wallerstein, *Capitalist Agriculture and the Origins of the European World-Economy in the Sixteenth Century*, vol. 1 of *The Modern World-System* (New York: Academic Press, 1974); Immanuel M. Wallerstein, *Mercantilism and the Consolidation of the European World-Economy, 1600–1750* (New York: Academic Press, 1980).

6   Abu-Lughod, *Cairo*.

7   Abu-Lughod and Hay, *Third World Urbanization*.

8   Abu-Lughod, *New York, Chicago, Los Angeles*; Abu-Lughod, *Race, Space, and Riots*.

9   Janet Abu-Lughod's Guggenheim Fellowship (http://www.gf.org/fellows/all-fellows/janet-l-abu-lughod-2/) and American Sociological Association Distinguished Career Award (http://www.asapews.org/awards.html) are noted on the respective organizations' websites.

SECTION 3
IMPACT

THE FIRST RESPONSES

KEY POINTS

- Although *Before European Hegemony* was favorably received by most sociologists and scholars of world-systems,* some historians were critical of its heavy reliance on secondary sources (that is, its frequent citation of previously written histories) and its numerous errors of fact and omission.

- Despite her muted response, Abu-Lughod welcomed criticism that contributed to the broader debate about the rise of the West.

- Shortly after the publication of *Before European Hegemony*, Abu-Lughod reviewed three studies on similar subjects that arrived at rather different conclusions. She argued that the differences were due to the eccentricities, ideologies, and idiosyncrasies of the authors, which she regarded as positive because they enabled different scholars to detect different patterns.

Criticism

The critical response to Janet Abu-Lughod's *Before European Hegemony: The World-System A.D. 1250–1350* was mainly favorable, if varied. Immanuel Wallerstein,* whose multi-volume work *The Modern World-System* encouraged Abu-Lughod to write her book,[1] applauded her account of the medieval world-system. "Perhaps specialists in each region will pick away at some of the detail," he observed, "but it will be hard to undermine the synthetic overview."[2] Although he questioned some of Abu-Lughod's language and reasoning, he agreed with her main arguments that the international

> **❝** Abu-Lughod's presentation overcomes one of the
> major disadvantages of much anti-Eurocentric writing.
> It is not just a loose collection of random exotica
> punctuated by outrage at the destructive Europeans,
> but a coherent explanation of how high agricultural
> productivity, an adequate manufacturing base, and
> well developed commercial techniques are necessary
> to sustain great civilizations and to keep them from
> becoming stagnant. **❞**
>
> Daniel Chirot, Review of *Before European Hegemony*

trade network of about 1300 C.E. constituted a world-system, that the collapse of the medieval system was a condition for the rise of the modern system, and that world-systems are by nature changeable.[3]

Sociologists and scholars of world-systems were generally more receptive to *Before European Hegemony* than scholars from other disciplines. The only review that brought a specific response from Abu-Lughod, however, was a detailed 17-page critique[4] from the sociologist Donald Nielsen,* who challenged Abu-Lughod's account on the grounds that it did not allow sufficient space for cultural explanations of different rates of development between different parts of the system. While Nielsen viewed Abu-Lughod's focus on cities as "one of the most welcome aspects of her book,"[5] he argued that her description of cities concealed wide variations between them. He also criticized Abu-Lughod's handling of chronology, her failure to recognize the importance of Europe's classical inheritance from ancient Greece and Rome, and her inaccurate and oversimplified representation of Max Weber's* thought.[6]

Historians were the harshest critics of *Before European Hegemony*. Some felt that Abu-Lughod was careless or selective in her presentation of the evidence. Archibald Lewis,* a scholar of medieval history, stated that "errors of fact, omissions of all sorts of relevant data, failure to mention whole regions of the world she is describing, and the tendency to mix evidence from periods centuries apart make this study of questionable value to the scholarly world."[7] Similarly, the historian Victor Lieberman* appreciated Abu-Lughod's description of the medieval world trading system but regarded her claim that the main sub-systems were equally capable of taking the next step into European-style modernity as "an article of faith."[8] The economic historian Avner Grief* saw the book as a useful introduction to a vast literature but otherwise dismissed it as "superficial if not misleading." Abu-Lughod's evidence failed to support her conclusions, he argued, and her insistence that the rise of the West depended on the decline of the East "skewed her historical research."[9] Others such as the American medieval historian Thomas Blomquist* and the prolific British scholar Norman Pounds* expressed reservations but were willing to accept the merits of a challenging, stimulating, and well-written book.[10]

Responses

Abu-Lughod welcomed criticism of *Before European Hegemony* but specifically responded only briefly to Nielsen's particularly unsympathetic review of her book. Despite its negative tone, Abu-Lughod saw the review as mainly favorable because it encouraged further research and debate on the rise of the West by pushing the study of world-systems back to the thirteenth century and broadening the geographical perspective to take fuller account of non-Western societies and their contributions. She wrote that she had purposely overemphasized "large-scale, systemic, geopolitical and economic factors" in the thirteenth and fourteenth century world-system because she believed that scholarship had underestimated them.[11] She sought to redress the balance by focusing on dimensions of the story that had not received sufficient attention.

In the preface to *Before European Hegemony*, Abu-Lughod addresses the criticism she expected for her reliance largely on secondary literature (accounts by other scholars) and very sparse use of primary sources (documents from the period being studied). Historians objected to Abu-Lughod's dependence on secondary sources because these sources sometimes obscured debate over the interpretation of the primary sources. Abu-Lughod remarks that her difficulty was precisely the opposite to that of specialist historians. The price of their concentration, she wrote, "is often a loss of peripheral vision."[12] In relying on the secondary literature, Abu-Lughod accepted that she was throwing herself "on the mercy of those who had devoted lifetimes to learning in depth what [she] could only know superficially."[13] Nowhere else did Abu-Lughod specifically respond to criticism of her book. She never published a second edition of *Before European Hegemony* and rarely revisited issues that she had raised in the book. Her later works focused mainly on three "global" cities in the United States—New York, Chicago, and Los Angeles.[14] This gave her little opportunity to consider questions arising from her book on the thirteenth-century world-system and critical reviews of it.

Conflict And Consensus

There is nothing to suggest that Abu-Lughod ever modified the views that she expressed in *Before European Hegemony* or that critics of her work changed their views. Many had doubts about some details of Abu-Lughod's arguments but most broadly agreed with her overview. Her main claims quickly entered into mainstream academic thought; the only claim that proved controversial was that the rise of the West in the modern system was based on the fall of the East in the medieval system.

Abu-Lughod touched upon some of the themes running through *Before European Hegemony* in her review of three studies on related subjects that appeared soon after her book; these accounts turned to similar secondary sources to arrive at different conclusions.[15] The difference, she wrote, stemmed from the role that scholarly imagination plays in writing synthetic history (that is, written history in which conclusions are founded on different sources). In particular, she defended the interplay of three human traits usually regarded as counterproductive to scholarly research—eccentricity, ideology, and idiosyncrasy (as opposed to objectivity, disinterest, and intersubjectivity)—because, she argued, they help scholars to distinguish patterns out of the mass of evidence that lay before them. Abu-Lughod viewed these "sins" not only as unavoidable but, when used with care, as enabling. They helped her to arrive at her vision of the multi-centered world-system of the thirteenth century and also explain why other scholars working on similar subjects at around the same time as her were able to reach such different conclusions.

NOTES

1   Immanuel M. Wallerstein, *Capitalist Agriculture and the Origins of the European World-Economy in the Sixteenth Century*, vol. 1 of *The Modern World-System* (New York: Academic Press, 1974); Immanuel M. Wallerstein, *Mercantilism and the Consolidation of the European World-Economy, 1600-1750*, vol. 2 of *The Modern World-System* (New York: Academic Press, 1980).

2   Immanuel M. Wallerstein, "Review of Janet Abu-Lughod, *Before European Hegemony*," *International Journal of Middle East Studies* 24 (1992): 129.

3   Wallerstein, "Review of Abu-Lughod, *Before European Hegemony*," 128–31.

4   Donald A. Nielsen, "After World Systems Theory: Concerning Janet Abu-Lughod's *Before European Hegemony*," *International Journal of Politics, Culture and Society* 4 (1991): 481–97; Janet L. Abu-Lughod, "Reply to Donald Nielsen's 'After World Systems Theory'," *International Journal of Politics, Culture and Society* 4 (1991): 499–500.

5   Nielsen, "After World Systems Theory," 487.

6   Nielsen, "After World Systems Theory," 493.

7   Archibald R. Lewis, "Review of Janet Abu-Lughod, *Before European Hegemony*," *Speculum* 66 (1991): 605–6.

8   Victor Lieberman, "Abu-Lughod's Egalitarian World Order: A Review Article," *Comparative Studies in Society and History* 35 (1993): 544–50.

9   Avner Grief, "Review of Janet Abu-Lughod, *Before European Hegemony*," *Journal of Economic History* 50 (1991): 455–6.

10 Thomas W. Blomquist, "Review of Janet Abu-Lughod, *Before European Hegemony*," *Business History Review* 64 (1990): 362–4. See also Norman J. G. Pounds, "Review of Janet Abu-Lughod, *Before European Hegemony*," *Annals of the Association of American Geographers* 81 (1991): 159–60; Beatrice F. Manz, "Review of Janet Abu-Lughod, *Before European Hegemony*," *Journal of Interdisciplinary History* 22 (1991): 101–3.

11 Abu-Lughod, "Reply to Donald Nielsen's After World Systems Theory"; Nielsen, "After World Systems Theory."

12 Janet L. Abu-Lughod, *Before European Hegemony: The World-System A.D. 1250–1350* (Oxford: Oxford University Press, 1989), ix.

13 Abu-Lughod, *Before European Hegemony*, xi.

14 Janet L. Abu-Lughod, *New York, Chicago, Los Angeles: America's Global Cities* (Minneapolis: University of Minnesota Press, 1999); Janet L. Abu-Lughod, *Race, Space, and Riots in Chicago, New York, and Los Angeles* (Oxford: Oxford University Press, 2007).

15 Janet L. Abu-Lughod, "The World-System Perspective in the Construction of Economic History," *History and Theory* 34 (1995): 86–98. For the books she discusses, respectively, see James M. Blaut, *1492: The Debate on Colonialism, Eurocentrism and History* (Trenton, NJ: Africa World Press, 1992); Alan K. Smith, *Creating a World Economy: Merchant Capital, Colonialism and World Trade, 1400–1825* (Boulder, CO: Westview Press, 1991); Jerry H. Bentley, *Old World Encounters: Cross-Cultural Contacts and Exchanges in Pre-Modern Times* (Oxford: Oxford University Press, 1993). She had previously reviewed the books by Smith and Bentley. See Janet L. Abu-Lughod, "Review of Creating a World Economy: Merchant Capital, Colonialism and World Trade, 1400–1825," *Contemporary Sociology* 21 (1992): 350–2; Janet L. Abu-Lughod, "Review of Old World Encounters: Cross-Cultural Contacts and Exchanges in Pre-Modern Times by Jerry H. Bentley," *American Historical Review* 99 (1994): 188–9.

MODULE 10
THE EVOLVING DEBATE

KEY POINTS

- Abu-Lughod's book encouraged other scholars to study world-systems* in place before 1500 and to consider more carefully the rise of the West after that date. New research in these areas nevertheless has generally lacked the broad geographical scope of *Before European Hegemony.*

- While the book's main idea that the hierarchical modern world-system grew out of an egalitarian medieval one is now widely accepted, some of the book's other themes are still debated.

- Although the book's impact on cutting-edge scholarship has been limited, it quickly became popular in university classrooms as a useful teaching text.

Uses And Problems

Janet Abu-Lughod's main argument in *Before European Hegemony: The World-System A.D. 1250–1350* was that the modern world-system described by Immanuel Wallerstein* was not the first such system but had evolved from a preexisting one.[1] Although other studies had pushed research on world-systems and the rise of the West back before the year 1500, *Before European Hegemony* was the first to do so on such a broad geographical scale. It encouraged other scholars to examine earlier world-systems and the rise of the West.[2] New work on world-systems before 1500 comparable in scale to that of Abu-Lughod nevertheless remains extremely rare. Much of the research on the Eurasian world-system before 1500 now tends to focus on specific individual parts of the system rather on than the system as a whole.[3]

> **❝** To explain Europe's subsequent hegemony,* it is necessary to look beyond her internal inventiveness and the virtues of her 'unique' entrepreneurial spirit. During the thirteenth century the other world powers had as promising a level of business acumen as, and an even more sophisticated set of economic institutions than, the Europeans. **❞**
>
> Janet Abu-Lughod, *Before European Hegemony: The World-System A.D. 1250–1350*

Abu-Lughod also emphasized the changeable nature of world-systems. She suggested that the modern world-system was evolving into a system more closely resembling the socially equal system of the Middle Ages than the hierarchical, European-dominated system of the last 500 years. She forecast that Asia would play a more important role in the new world-system—an idea that other scholars have continued to develop.[4] Most importantly, Abu-Lughod argued that major cities constituted the points of contact between different parts of the medieval world-system. Most of the system was agricultural and subsistence-oriented, but key cities formed an "archipelago" of "world cities."*[5] Within specific areas, these cities exercised hegemony.* They drained surplus production and resources from their hinterlands* and from satellite cities and towns; they also oversaw the organization of production and labor that was necessary for export to be possible and, within the areas around them, determined the rules of engagement in the wider economy. Although no one else has gone on to study world cities in the medieval world-system, Abu-Lughod's book gave rise to the new sub-discipline of world-city analysis in the context of world-systems.[6]

Schools Of Thought

It is difficult to identify any well-defined school of thought associated with Janet Abu-Lughod's *Before European Hegemony*. The book's central premise that the modern world-system arose from the residue of an earlier system in which three main sub-systems in Europe, the Middle East, and Asia interacted more or less equitably is now widely accepted. The argument has not undergone significant further development, and scholarly debate has taken little account of some of Abu-Lughod's other claims, such as that there was no inherent reason why the West came to dominate the modern world-system, or that the rise of the West starting around 1500 depended on the fall of the East.

Before European Hegemony has been most influential in the study of world cities in the context of world-systems. When Abu-Lughod actively began her research on the medieval world-system, she had already published two major works on cities in opposite corners of North Africa—one on Cairo in Egypt, and another on Rabat in Morocco.[7] In the meantime, she had also co-edited an important collection of writings on cities in the developing world.[8] Her background in urban studies led her to concentrate on key cities in her description of the medieval world-system. She focused in particular on the "archipelago" of "world cities" that were the chief points of contact between different parts of the system. Even the most strident critics of *Before European Hegemony* were excited about this part of her work,[9] which encouraged further research on the role and function of cities in world-systems.[10] Abu-Lughod went on to consider the place of New York, Chicago, and Los Angeles in the modern world-system, confirming her reputation as a leading scholar of world cities in the context of world-systems.[11]

In Current Scholarship

Few scholars have taken up the project that Abu-Lughod started in *Before European Hegemony*. There has not been any comprehensive reconsideration of the international trade network in Europe, the Middle East, and Asia during the thirteenth and fourteenth centuries that gives equal space to all three main regions. This reflects the enormous proportions of Abu-Lughod's original project and the difficulties involved in a thorough reassessment. Abu-Lughod addressed the most manageable questions concerning the existence and structure of the medieval world-system. Her explanations of more troublesome issues, such as the breakdown of the medieval system and the transition to the European-dominated modern system, have proved insufficient or inadequate to stimulate further debate on the same geographical scale.

Scholars have examined aspects of Abu-Lughod's project; they have generally studied individual parts of the medieval system or developed themes that she introduced. Later research has considered, for example, the place of Asia in the world-system since 1400 and the importance of maritime trade on the Indian Ocean in integrating its regions into the Eurasian and African world-systems before 1500.[12] Other studies have examined the role and function of world cities in the context of world-systems.[13] The impact of Abu-Lughod's book on doctoral students has been limited. Her graduate students at Northwestern University and the New School for Social Research generally pursued dissertations on subjects other than world-systems analysis—mostly on urban development.[14] On rare occasions when they have studied world-systems, they considered the development of particular places within the context of the world-system.[15] Other dissertations on world-systems in English completed since the publication of *Before European Hegemony* have focused mostly on aspects of the modern world-system described by Wallerstein.[16]

Only a few doctoral students have written dissertations on world-systems pre-dating the year 1500, generally on a far more limited geographical scale.[17] Abu-Lughod's book has had greater impact in the classroom, where it quickly developed a reputation as a valuable teaching text.

NOTES

1 Immanuel M. Wallerstein, *Capitalist Agriculture and the Origins of the European World-Economy in the Sixteenth Century*, vol. 1 of *The Modern World-System* (New York: Academic Press, 1974); Immanuel M. Wallerstein, *Mercantilism and the Consolidation of the European World-Economy, 1600–1750*, vol. 2 of *The Modern World-System* (New York: Academic Press, 1980).

2 Andre Gunder Frank and Barry K. Gills, *The World System: Five Hundred Years or Five Thousand?* (London: Routledge, 1993); Christopher Chase-Dunn and Thomas D. Hall, *Rise and Demise: Comparing World-Systems* (Boulder, CO: Westview Press, 1997); Eric Mielants, *The Origins of Capitalism and the "Rise of the West"* (Philadelphia: Temple University Press, 2007).

3 For example, see Philippe Beaujard, "The Indian Ocean in Eurasian and African World-Systems before the Sixteenth Century," *Journal of World History* 16 (2005): 411–65.

4 Most notably, see Andre Gunder Frank, *ReOrient: Global Economy in the Asian Age* (Berkeley: University of California Press, 1998). See also Tanaka Akihiko, *The New Middle Ages: The World System in the 21st Century*, trans. Jean Connell Hoff (Tokyo: International House of Japan, 2002), which seems to draw substantially on ideas expressed in *Before European Hegemony* about the rise of Asia in the new world-system without actually citing Abu-Lughod's book.

5 Janet L. Abu-Lughod, *Before European Hegemony: The World System A.D. 1250–1350* (Oxford: Oxford University Press, 1989), 13–14, 32–3, 353. On world cities per se, see John Friedmann and Goetz Wolff, "World City Formation," *International Journal of Urban and Regional Research* 4 (1980): 309–43.

6 For example, see Saskia Sassen, *Cities in a World Economy* (Thousand Oaks, CA: Pine Forge Press, 1994); Andrew Bosworth, "World-Cities and World Economic Cycles," in *Civilisations and World Systems: Studying World-Historical Change*, ed. Stephen K. Sanderson (Walnut Creek, CA: Altamira Press, 1995), 206–27; Peter L. Knox and Peter J. Taylor, eds, *World-Cities in a World-System* (Cambridge: Cambridge University Press, 1995).

7 Janet L. Abu-Lughod, *Cairo: 1001 Years of the City Victorious* (Princeton, NJ: Princeton University Press, 1971); Janet L. Abu-Lughod, *Rabat: Urban Apartheid in Morocco* (Princeton, NJ: Princeton University Press, 1980).

8 Janet L. Abu-Lughod and Richard A. Hay Jr., eds, *Third World Urbanization* (Chicago: Maaroufa Press, 1977).

9   Donald A. Nielsen, "After World Systems Theory: Concerning Janet Abu-Lughod's *Before European Hegemony*," *International Journal of Politics, Culture and Society* 4 (1991): 487–9.

10 For example, see Sassen, *Cities in a World Economy*; Bosworth, "World-Cities and World Economic Cycles"; Knox and Taylor, *World-cities in a World-System*.

11 Janet L. Abu-Lughod, *New York, Chicago, Los Angeles: America's Global Cities* (Minneapolis: University of Minnesota Press, 1999).

12 Frank, *ReOrient*; Beaujard, "The Indian Ocean."

13 Sassen, *Cities in a World Economy*; Knox and Taylor, *World-Cities in a World-System*.

14 For example, Christopher Mele, "Reinventing the East Village of New York: Capitalist Investment Strategies, 1860–1990" (PhD diss., New School for Social Research, 1994).

15 Gerardo del Cerro Santamaría, "Bilbao and Globalisation: Transnational Networks, Political Economy, and Urban Restructuring in a City on the Global Map" (PhD diss., New School for Social Research, 2003).

16 For example, Steven Marc Sherman, "Hegemonic Transitions and Cultural Change: The Making and Unmaking of Hegemonic Modernity in the Modern World System" (PhD diss., State University of New York, 1999); Miin-Wen Shih, "The Rise of China in a World-System Perspective" (PhD diss., State University of New York, 2001); Joseph Price Moore III, "Native Americans in Colonial New England and the Modern World-System" (PhD diss., Rutgers State University of New Jersey, 2011). See also Wallerstein, *Capitalist Agriculture* and *Mercantilism*.

17 Most notably Alice Louise Willard, "Rivers of Gold, Oceans of Sand: The Songhay in the West African World-System" (PhD diss., Johns Hopkins University, 1999).

MODULE 11
IMPACT AND INFLUENCE TODAY

KEY POINTS

- *Before European Hegemony* is a useful teaching text for undergraduate and graduate courses in medieval history and world history* that has receded from the cutting edge of scholarship.

- The text continues to raise questions about the transition from the medieval world-system* to the modern one and the rise of the West.

- Responses to Abu-Lughod's argument that the rise of the West depended on the fall of the East have varied from defending the unique character of the West to silence.

Position

Janet Abu-Lughod's *Before European Hegemony* no longer plays a major role in scholarly debates. Its principal arguments are that the modern world-system described by Immanuel Wallerstein* arose from the ruins of a preexisting system and that the hierarchical structure of the modern system was not the only possible structure of world-systems.[1] These claims quickly entered into mainstream academic thought.

Abu-Lughod also argues that the medieval system broke down after the middle of the fourteenth century due to the collapse of the so-called *Pax Mongolica* (Mongol Peace)* in Asia and the catastrophic spread of the plague remembered as the Black Death.* The breakdown was more profound in the East, however, and Europeans adapted more easily to the changing circumstances. According to Abu-Lughod, the rise of the West in the modern world-system depended on the more complete collapse of the East in the medieval system. This claim lacks the widespread appeal of

> ❝ The thesis of this book is that there was no *inherent historical necessity* that shifted the system to favor the West rather than the East, nor was there any inherent historical necessity that would have prevented cultures in the eastern region from becoming the progenitors of the modern world system. ❞
>
> Janet Abu-Lughod, *Before European Hegemony: The World-System A.D. 1250–1350*

the author's main arguments and it was so weakly developed that it failed to attract debate and was largely ignored or forgotten.

Before European Hegemony pushed world-systems analysis back to the thirteenth century, tied the emergence of the modern system to the disintegration of the medieval one, and "cut into the Gordian knot of the supposed break in world history around 1500."[2] The book's multidisciplinary approach, broad geographical scope, and attention to both subaltern* and dominant perspectives also followed existing trends in academic fashion and contributed to its appeal. The continuing importance of the book today derives from its popularity as a useful teaching text that engages with perennial questions about the origins of capitalism,* the revival of cities in medieval Europe, and the rise of the West. "Presenting this book to students," wrote one reviewer, "is an excellent idea," because it shocks them "into awareness that there were great civilizations in the past" interacting with each other in large-scale networks.[3] The 53-page bibliography also provides an excellent introduction to the pre-1989 literature on cities and trade in the medieval world-system for non–specialists.

Interaction

Before European Hegemony challenged Wallerstein's survey of the European-dominated modern world-system.[4] Abu-Lughod agrees that the modern system existed in the way that Wallerstein described it, but questions both his claim that it was the first such system and the implication that the hierarchical structure of the system was the only possible structure for world-systems. Initially, Wallerstein believed that earlier systems were bound together by the structures of empire rather than by the demands of commercial exchange between independent entities. Such systems, he felt, could not be called world-systems. Focusing on major cities, or "world cities,"* however, Abu-Lughod shows that independent economies in medieval Europe, the Middle East, and Asia traded fairly equitably with each other, whether directly or indirectly. This suggested an alternative structure to the hierarchical one that Wallerstein proposed for the modern system. While Wallerstein differed with Abu-Lughod on points of detail, he later agreed that the modern world-system was not the first of its kind and that the hierarchical structure of the modern system was not the only possible structure of world-systems.[5]

Abu-Lughod's exploration of the world-system before 1500 inspired other scholars to study earlier systems and to recognize their capitalist* or pre-capitalist features.[6] Her focus on the structural differences between the medieval and modern systems encouraged scholars to analyze evolutionary processes more closely. Recent research has considered, for example, the collapse of the Soviet* world-system, the integration of peripheral parts of a system, and the sequence of hegemonies.*[7] Abu-Lughod's examination of the thirteenth-century world-system through the prism of key cities also helped to foster the sub-discipline of world-city analysis in the context of world systems,[8] in which she took a leading role.[9]

Before European Hegemony even helped to set the stage for the launch by Christopher Chase-Dunn* of the *Journal of World-Systems Research** in 1995.[10] The book contributed to debates in world history over periodization and structure by stressing the importance of taking into balanced account both dominant and subaltern perspectives—that is, the importance of acknowledging, for example, that the term "medieval" may mean one thing in reference to European history but something a little different in reference to the history of the Far East.[11]

The Continuing Debate

Abu-Lughod's main arguments in *Before European Hegemony* quickly entered into mainstream academic thought, but some of her secondary claims have failed to provoke further debate. She devotes so much of her book to the description of the medieval world-system that little space remains to consider the transition of the medieval system to the modern one. She argues that the rise of the West in the modern system depended on the collapse of the East in the medieval one in just a few pages in the concluding chapter, leaving her ideas on this subject weakly developed. This meant that they didn't spark the interest of other scholars, and the transition from the egalitarian medieval world-system to the European-dominated modern one therefore remains poorly understood and little studied.

Other themes that Abu-Lughod also discusses only briefly in *Before European Hegemony* have attracted greater attention and continue to play a part in today's debates. Her predictions about the growing importance of Asia in the further evolution of the modern world-system helped to encourage new research on Asia's changing position in the system.[12] By studying the thirteenth-century world-system through the prism of key cities, moreover, she helped to give rise to a new sub-discipline—namely, world-city analysis in the context of world-systems—of which she became a leading scholar.[13] There is little evidence, however, of continuing debate against the ideas that Abu-Lughod expressed in her book.

NOTES

1   Immanuel M. Wallerstein, *Capitalist Agriculture and the Origins of the European World-Economy in the Sixteenth Century*, vol. 1 of *The Modern World-System* (New York: Academic Press, 1974); Immanuel M. Wallerstein, *Mercantilism and the Consolidation of the European World-Economy, 1600–1750*, vol. 2 of *The Modern World-System* (New York: Academic Press, 1980).

2   Andre Gunder Frank, "The Thirteenth-Century World-System: A Review Essay," *Journal of World History* 1 (1990): 249–56, quoted from 249.

3   Daniel Chirot, "Was Europe Lucky, Evil or Smart? Review of Janet Abu-Lughod, *Before European Hegemony*," *Comparative Sociology* 20 (1991): 26–8.

4   Wallerstein, *Capitalist Agriculture*; Wallerstein, *Mercantilism*.

5   Immanuel M. Wallerstein, "Review of Janet Abu-Lughod, *Before European Hegemony*," *International Journal of Middle East Studies* 24 (1992): 128–31.

6   Andre Gunder Frank and Barry K. Gills, *The World System: Five Hundred Years or Five Thousand?* (London: Routledge, 1993); Christopher Chase-Dunn and Thomas D. Hall, *Rise and Demise: Comparing World-Systems* (Boulder, CO: Westview Press, 1997); Philippe Beaujard, "The Indian Ocean in Eurasian and African World-Systems before the Sixteenth Century," *Journal of World History* 16 (2005): 411–65; Eric Mielants, *The Origins of Capitalism and the "Rise of the West"* (Philadelphia: Temple University Press, 2007); Elizabeth Ann Pollard, "Placing Greco-Roman History in World Historical Context," *The Classical World* 102 (2008): 53–68.

7   Respectively, Mikhail Balaev, "The Effects of International Trade on Democracy: A Panel Study of the Post-Soviet World-System," *Sociological Perspectives* 52 (2009): 337–62; Rob Clark, "World-System Mobility and Economic Growth, 1980–2000," *Social Forces* 88 (2010): 1123–51; Roy Kown, "Hegemonies in the World-System: An Empirical Assessment of Hegemonic Sequences from the 16th to 20th Century," *Sociological Perspectives* 54 (2011): 593–617.

8   Saskia Sassen, *Cities in a World Economy* (Thousand Oaks, CA: Pine Forge Press, 1994); Peter L. Knox and Peter J. Taylor, eds, *World-Cities in a World-System* (Cambridge: Cambridge University Press, 1995). On the study of world cities per se, see John Friedmann and Goetz Wolff, "World City Formation," *International Journal of Urban and Regional Research* 4 (1980): 309–43.

9   Janet L. Abu-Lughod, *New York, Chicago, Los Angeles: America's Global Cities* (Minneapolis: University of Minnesota Press, 1999).

10 *Journal of World-Systems Research* (Riverside, CA: Institute for Research on World-Systems, 1995–).

11 William A. Green, "Periodization in European and World History," *Journal of World History* 3 (1992): 13–53; William A. Green, "Periodizing World History," *History and Theory* 34 (1995): 99–111; Jerry H. Bentley, "Cross-Cultural Interaction and Periodization in World History," *American Historical Review* 101 (1996): 749–70.

12 Andre Gunder Frank, *ReOrient: Global Economy in the Asian Age* (Berkeley: University of California Press, 1998); Tanaka Akihiko, *The New Middle Ages: The World System in the 21st Century*, trans. Jean Connell Hoff (Tokyo: International House of Japan, 2002).

13 Sassen, *Cities in a World Economy*; Knox and Taylor, *World-Cities in a World-System*; Abu-Lughod, *New York, Chicago, Los Angeles*. On the study of world cities per se, see John Friedmann and Goetz Wolff, "World City Formation."

WHERE NEXT?

KEY POINTS

- *Before European Hegemony* is an innovative contribution to the study of world-systems.* It is likely to remain important as a university teaching text, even if its impact on scholarship has been limited, in part because of its heavy reliance on secondary sources.

- The text encourages classroom debate and engages with perennial questions about the rise of the West and the origins of capitalism.*

- The book remains a pioneering study of the Eurasian trade network, devoting equal attention to the European, Middle Eastern, and Asian parts of the system.

Potential

The lasting significance of Janet Abu-Lughod's *Before European Hegemony: The World-System A.D. 1250–1350* is likely to be greatest in university classrooms. Within just a few years of its publication, it secured a place on undergraduate and graduate syllabuses as a useful teaching text, especially in world history* and medieval history. Its broad geographical scale and comparative, multidisciplinary approach are well suited for encouraging classroom discussion and critical analysis. The book also engages with the theories of leading thinkers such as the economist and social philosopher Karl Marx,* the Belgian historian Henri Pirenne,* and the influential German sociologist Max Weber* on long-standing questions about the origins of capitalism and the rise of the West. Although the growth of courses in which world history is taught

> **❝** In a system, it is the *connections* between the parts that must be studied. When these strengthen and reticulate [form a pattern], the system may be said to 'rise'; when they fray, the system declines, although it may later undergo reorganization and revitalization. **❞**
>
> Janet Abu-Lughod, *Before European Hegemony: The World-System A.D. 1250–1350*

further contributed to the book's popularity, its future outside the classroom is difficult to predict.

Before European Hegemony was an innovative contribution to the new discipline of world-systems analysis because it pushed the study of world-systems back before 1500, stressed the evolutionary character of world-systems, focused on the key role of world cities* in facilitating exchange between the different sub-systems, and described the medieval system in a way that gave a balanced account of dominant and subaltern* perspectives. It also gave rise to a new sub-discipline, world-city analysis within the context of world-systems, of which Abu-Lughod became a leading scholar.[1] Its impact on later research has nevertheless been relatively modest, especially in historical studies, due largely to the author's heavy and sometimes uncritical reliance on secondary sources—that is, on literature written by other historians about the period as opposed to original documents from the time under study.

Future Directions

Before European Hegemony grew out of Janet Abu-Lughod's deep interest in cities and their interrelationships. As she explored these interrelationships, she was increasingly struck by the ways in which they both influenced production and the organization of labor in and around cities and determined the shape of the overall system. She continued to focus on cities in her later work, which was on the three largest cities in the United States, confirming her reputation as a leading scholar of world cities in the context of world-systems.[2] Another important aspect of Abu-Lughod's book was its recognition of the evolutionary character of world-systems—the fact that they are dynamic systems that are in constant change—though she may not have carried this point far enough. Her emphasis on the Black Death* as triggering the collapse of the thirteenth-century world-system, for example, perhaps led her to downplay or even ignore important continuities between the medieval and modern systems. There may yet be scope for further study of the transition from the medieval system to the modern one.

The ideas that Abu-Lughod expressed in *Before European Hegemony* failed to give rise to a distinct school of thought or group of followers. The book in fact marked a distinct turning point in Abu-Lughod's career. Before its publication, she had focused on cities in the developing world, mainly in the Middle East and North Africa.[3] Afterwards, she turned her attention to the study of world cities in the developed world, particularly in the United States.[4] Her graduate students at Northwestern University and the New School for Social Research wrote dissertations on subjects other than world-systems analysis, mostly on urban development,[5] though sometimes within the context of the broader world-system.[6]

Most English-language dissertations on world-systems completed since the publication of *Before European Hegemony* have focused on aspects of the modern world-system described by Wallerstein.[7] Only a few doctoral students have written dissertations on world-systems pre-dating the year 1500.[8] Even in the flourishing literature on world cities in the context of world-systems, most scholarship focuses on relatively recent developments. The future of *Before European Hegemony* rests above all on its use as a teaching text in university classrooms.

Summary

Abu-Lughod's *Before European Hegemony* weaves together the history of Europe, the Middle East, and Asia during the century or so before the Black Death. The geographical scope of the work, the roughly equal treatment that it accords all three regions in terms of both space and perspective, and its emphasis on the connections between the three regions are all highly unusual in a book on medieval history. Abu-Lughod's book effectively situates important aspects of medieval European, Middle Eastern, and Asian history within the broader context of the world-system. It also combines a global perspective with an approach to the study of the thirteenth-century world-system that balances dominant perspectives with subaltern views. Perhaps its most original feature is its examination of the world-system of around 1300 through the prism of world cities and its description, borrowed via Fernand Braudel from the German historian Rudolf Häpke, of the "international" trade network of the period as an "archipelago of towns."

Before European Hegemony deserves attention as a provocative examination of the medieval world-system in direct response to the first two installments of Immanuel Wallerstein's* multi-volume survey of the modern world-system (published between 1974 and 2011).[9] Abu-Lughod's book compelled scholars to acknowledge the existence of world-systems before the rise of Wallerstein's modern system. It also undermined the implication that the hierarchical structure of Wallerstein's European-dominated system was the only possible structure of world-systems. At the same time, Abu-Lughod focused on key cities as points of contact between the various parts of the wider system. She also exploited the opportunity to consider enduring questions about the origins of capitalism, the rise of the West, and the role of cities in economic development. The ongoing appeal of the book indeed derives, above all, from the fact that it is a useful teaching text written in simple, straightforward language.

NOTES

1   Saskia Sassen, *Cities in a World Economy* (Thousand Oaks, CA: Pine Forge Press, 1994); Peter L. Knox and Peter J. Taylor, eds, *World-Cities in a World-System* (Cambridge: Cambridge University Press, 1995); Janet L. Abu-Lughod, *New York, Chicago, Los Angeles: America's Global Cities* (Minneapolis: University of Minnesota Press, 1999). On the study of world cities per se, see John Friedmann and Goetz Wolff, "World City Formation," *International Journal of Urban and Regional Research* 4 (1980): 309–43.

2   Abu-Lughod, *New York, Chicago, Los Angeles*.

3   Janet L. Abu-Lughod, *Cairo: 1001 Years of the City Victorious* (Princeton, NJ: Princeton University Press, 1971); Janet L. Abu-Lughod and Richard A. Hay, eds, *Third World Urbanization* (Chicago: Maaroufa Press, 1977); Janet L. Abu-Lughod, *Rabat: Urban Apartheid in Morocco* (Princeton, NJ: Princeton University Press, 1980).

4   Janet L. Abu-Lughod et al., *From Urban Village to East Village: The Battle for New York's Lower East Side* (Oxford: Basil Blackwell, 1994); Abu-Lughod, *New York, Chicago, Los Angeles*; Janet L. Abu-Lughod, *Race, Space, and Riots in Chicago, New York, and Los Angeles* (Oxford: Oxford University Press, 2007).

5   For example, Christopher Mele, "Reinventing the East Village of New York: Capitalist Investment Strategies, 1860–1990" (PhD diss., New School for Social Research, 1994).

6   For example, Gerardo del Cerro Santamaría, "Bilbao and Globalisation: Transnational Networks, Political Economy, and Urban Restructuring in a City on the Global Map" (PhD diss., New School for Social Research, 2003).

7   Steven Marc Sherman, "Hegemonic Transitions and Cultural Change: The Making and Unmaking of Hegemonic Modernity in the Modern World System" (PhD diss., State University of New York, 1999); Miin-Wen Shih, "The Rise of China in a World-System Perspective" (PhD diss., State University of New York, 2001); Joseph Price Moore III, "Native Americans in Colonial New England and the Modern World-System" (PhD diss., Rutgers State University of New Jersey, 2011). See also Immanuel M. Wallerstein, *Capitalist Agriculture and the Origins of the European World-Economy in the Sixteenth Century*, vol. 1. of *The Modern World-System* (New York: Academic Press, 1974); Immanuel M. Wallerstein, *Mercantilism and the Consolidation of the European World-Economy, 1600–1750*, vol. 2 of *The Modern World-System* (New York: Academic Press, 1980).

8   Most notably Alice Louise Willard, "Rivers of Gold, Oceans of Sand: The Songhay in the West African World-System" (PhD diss., Johns Hopkins University, 1999).

9   Wallerstein, *Capitalist Agriculture*; Wallerstein, *Mercantilism*.

GLOSSARY

GLOSSARY OF TERMS

Annales school of history: a school of historians that emerged in France with the introduction of the journal *Annales*, founded by the French historians Marc Bloch and Lucien Febvre in 1929. The *Annales* school developed a multidisciplinary approach to historical study that borrowed from the social sciences, emphasized the underlying structures of history rather than individual actors and key events, and acknowledged the importance of geography and climate in history.

Berlin Wall: a barrier erected by the East German government (German Democratic Republic, or GDR) in 1961 that enclosed West Berlin and separated it from East Germany and East Berlin, making it easier to control movement into and out of West Berlin. In 1989, during a wave of civil unrest that spread across Eastern Europe, the GDR eased restrictions on the movement of its citizens into West Berlin and then dismantled the wall against the backdrop of the reunification of East and West Germany.

Black Death: a major pandemic plague that spread from Central Asia to Europe in the mid-fourteenth century, reaching Mediterranean Europe by the end of 1347 and England in 1348. The source of infection was the bacterium *Yersinia pestis*, which was carried by rodent-borne fleas that transmitted the disease to humans. The fourteenth-century plague probably killed 50 percent or more of the populations of crowded cities and 20–30 percent of rural inhabitants.

Capitalism: defined variously by economists, historians, and sociologists, this is generally understood as an economic system characterized by private ownership of most trade and industry in which private firms generally operate to generate a profit. Private property, wage labor, investment for profit, and competition are typical features of capitalist economies.

Cold War: a period of heightened tension between the United States and its allies in the North American Treaty Organization (NATO) on the one hand and the Soviet Union, together with its satellites in Eastern Europe and China, on the other, lasting from the end of World War II in 1945 until the dissolution of the Soviet Union in 1991.

Communist: here, this term refers to the regimes established in the Soviet Union in 1922, in Central and Eastern Europe after 1945, and in China in 1949 in which productive property was nationalized and placed under strict government control.

Dependency theory: the process according to which developed "core" countries draw resources from lesser-developed countries that occupy the "periphery" of the world-system, to the benefit of the core countries and detriment of the peripheral ones. The poverty that is characteristic of peripheral countries, according to the theory, stems more from the way in which they are integrated into the world economy than from the absence of economic integration.

Feudalism: a socioeconomic system that regulated relationships among the military aristocracy in Europe during the Middle Ages (the period from the ninth to the fifteenth centuries C.E.) In this system, landholding nobles (lords) granted lands (fiefs) to others who were lower down in the social order (vassals) in exchange for military service, labor, or a portion of the produce from the land.

Hegemony: the authority, dominance, or influence exercised by one group over others, particularly with respect to economic and political relations between countries or regions.

Hinterland: the rural area immediately surrounding large cities, especially commercially oriented port cities; it has close economic relations with the parent city, depending on the city for imported goods and services while providing the city with essential resources for industry and with staple food supplies for the large non-agrarian population.

Journal of World-Systems Research: sometimes abbreviated as *JWSR*, this is an open-access, peer-reviewed journal founded in 1995 by American sociologist Christopher Chase-Dunn and dedicated to the study of world-systems.

Marxism: the economic, political, and social theories put forward in the nineteenth century by the economist and social theorist Karl Marx* and the social scientist Friedrich Engels in which class struggle between the proletariat (workers) and the bourgeoisie (capitalists who own and control the means of production) is seen as the dominant force in history.

Mongol Peace (*Pax Mongolica*): the long period of stability that prevailed in Asia during the thirteenth and early fourteenth centuries as a result of the expansion of the Mongol Empire under Genghis Kahn (c.1162–1227) and his successors and the political unification of a large part of Asia. International trade and cultural exchange between Europe and the Mongol Empire flourished in this period, but the empire began to disintegrate in the fourteenth century and trade between the East and West declined.

Mongols: a Central Asian people native to the area that is present-day Mongolia and parts of what is today China.

Soviet Union, or Union of Soviet Socialist Republics (USSR): a highly centralized Marxist–Leninist state made up of the subnational territories of the old Russian Empire in Eastern Europe and Asia. It formed after the Bolshevik Revolution of 1917, which precipitated the collapse of Tsarist Russia, and took definitive shape in 1922. The Soviet Union collapsed in 1991 and dissolved into 15 separate states.

Subaltern: a term that originally referred to a person or group of inferior rank or status but that now is commonly used to refer to marginalized or oppressed classes or members of society, in contrast to the hegemonic, or dominant, classes or members.

Tiananmen Square: a city square in central Beijing that takes its name from the Tiananmen Gate to the north, which leads to the Forbidden City. In early June 1989, after several weeks of student protests in the square, Chinese government troops moved in on the square to enforce martial law and forcibly suppressed the protests.

World cities: major cities that mediate trade in the international trade network. Some of these cities are commercial enclaves without hinterlands, but most are able to draw on resources and labor from the surrounding area. An important characteristic of world cities with hinterlands is that production and labor in the hinterland are organized to meet the needs of the export market.

World history: also called global history or transnational history, this is the study of history on a global scale, taking into account the perspectives of both dominant and subaltern (marginalized) sections of society. The rise of world history as a distinct academic field was marked by the birth of the World History Association in 1982, the creation of graduate programs in world history at several American universities in the ensuing years, and the introduction of the *Journal of World History* in 1990.

World-systems analysis: a multidisciplinary field of research that uses the research tools and methodologies of the social sciences to examine world history and social change beyond the level of the nation-state, usually in terms of the distribution of wealth and division of labor between core countries (the United States, Western Europe, Japan), those on the semi-periphery (developing countries such as Brazil, China, and India), and those on the periphery (lesser-developed countries, including much of Africa).

World War II: the global conflict that took place between 1939 and 1945, with Germany, Italy, and Japan (the Axis powers) on one side, and Britain, the Soviet Union, the United States, and other nations (the Allies) on the other.

PEOPLE MENTIONED IN THE TEXT

Thomas Blomquist (1931–2007) was an American historian
of thirteenth-century Italian trade and banking who focused on
merchant-banking families in the Tuscan city of Lucca. He was
professor of history at Northern Illinois University in DeKalb, Illinois,
where he taught for 32 years from the mid-1960s until his retirement
in the 1990s.

Fernand Braudel (1902–85) was a French historian, leader of the
so-called *Annales* school of history, and author of *The Mediterranean
and the Mediterranean World in the Age of Philip II* (1972–73), which
he originally drafted from memory while he was a prisoner of war
in Germany during World War II.* Braudel later wrote a major
three-volume synthesis entitled *Civilization and Capitalism, 15th–18th
Centuries* (1979).

Christopher Chase-Dunn (b. 1944) is an American sociologist,
scholar, and author, specializing in world-systems. He founded the
Institute for Research on World-Systems at the University of California
and is the founding editor of the *Journal of World-Systems Research*.

Andre Gunder Frank (1929–2005) was a German American
economic historian, social scientist, and early pioneer of dependency
theory, which holds that underdeveloped states become trapped in
their relationship with developed states, providing resources and
inexpensive labor to them while serving as markets for them and
outlets for their obsolete technology. Frank also stressed the
importance of economic power in determining a nation's position
in the world order, while making significant contributions, too, to
world-systems analysis.

Avner Grief (b. 1955) is an American economic historian and professor of economics at Stanford University in California. His research focuses on the role of social institutions in economic development in Europe and the Middle East during the Middle Ages. He is the author of *Institutions and the Path to the Modern Economy: Lessons from Medieval Trade* (2006).

Thomas S. Kuhn (1922–96) was a physicist and historian of science who is best known as the author of *The Structure of Scientific Revolutions* (1961), a controversial and influential work, now in its fourth edition. His other books include *The Copernican Revolution: Planetary Astronomy in the Development of Western Thought* (1957) and *Black Body Theory and the Quantum Discontinuity, 1894–1912* (1978).

Archibald R. Lewis (1914–90) was an American historian and author of ten books and numerous articles mostly on the seas, naval power, and maritime trade in Europe and the Mediterranean during the Middle Ages, including interaction between the East and West. Educated at Princeton University, Lewis taught at the University of Texas at Austin and the University of Massachusetts.

Victor Lieberman (b. 1945) is an American historian of Southeast Asia and the author of several books and numerous articles. He is the Raoul Wallenberg Distinguished University Professor and Professor of Asian and Comparative History at the University of Michigan in Ann Arbor.

Maurice Lombard (1904–65) was a French historian, born in Algeria, who specialized in the economic history of the Islamic world during the Early Middle Ages. His best-known work, *The Golden Age of Islam* (1975), was first published posthumously in French in 1971.

Karl Marx (1818–83) was a German scholar who is best known for his contributions to socialism and social science, above all economics, and for his model of class struggle referred to as Marxism. In 1848, he published *The Manifesto of the Communist Party* with German social scientist and political theorist Friedrich Engels (1820–95); later he wrote his major three-volume work on political economy, *Capital* (1867–94).

William McNeill (b. 1917) is a Canadian-born American historian who pioneered the study of particular subjects and themes on a global scale across huge sweeps of time, helping to establish world history as a distinct academic discipline. One of his early books, *The Rise of the West* (1963), focused on the interaction between civilizations and the effect of Western civilization on other societies.

Lewis Mumford (1895–1990) was a historian, sociologist, philosopher of technology, and literary critic, as well as a columnist for *The New Yorker* magazine. He wrote on cities and urbanization, won the US National Book Award in 1962 for *The City in History*, and was awarded the Presidential Medal of Freedom in 1964.

Donald A. Nielsen is a sociologist and scholar of religion. He is the author of two books, including *Three Faces of God: Society, Religion and the Categories of Totality in the Philosophy of Emile Durkheim* (1999), and numerous articles. He taught sociology and religion at the State University of New York at Oneonta, the University of Wisconsin–Eau Claire, and the College of Charleston in South Carolina.

Henri Pirenne (1862–1935) was a Belgian historian of Europe and the Middle Ages who identified the key break in European history with the spread of Islam in the seventh and eighth centuries rather than with the fall of the Roman Empire in the fifth century, thus rejecting the pivotal role of the barbarian invasions of the fifth and sixth centuries. Pirenne's ideas about the development of Europe in the Middle Ages, collectively referred to as the Pirenne Thesis, are expressed in his works *Medieval Cities: Their Origins and the Revival of Trade* (1928) and the posthumous *Mohammed and Charlemagne* (1937).

Karl Polanyi (1886–1964) was a Hungarian scholar who was best known for his work in economic anthropology and whose research on markets, money, and trade stressed that early, non-market economies were "embedded" in their social and cultural contexts and could not be studied independently. Polanyi's major works include *The Great Transformation* (1944), on the interrelated development of the modern state and market capitalism in nineteenth-century Britain, and *Trade and Markets in Early Empires* (1957).

Norman J. G. Pounds (1912–2006) was a British historian and geographer who wrote more than 30 books on European history and geography, covering a wide range of subjects from antiquity to the present. From 1950 to 1977, he taught geography at Indiana University in Bloomington, Indiana.

Joseph Schumpeter (1883–1950) was an Austrian economist who had published groundbreaking works on theoretical economics and the history of economic theory by the age of 31. He later wrote an ambitious study titled *Business Cycles* (1939) and followed that with *Capitalism, Socialism, and Democracy* (1942), his most famous contribution to economics, which introduced the concept of "creative destruction" and explained the importance of entrepreneurship to economic development.

Immanuel Wallerstein (b. 1930) is an American historical sociologist, author of more than 20 books, and syndicated columnist on world affairs. From 1976 to 2005, as a distinguished professor of sociology at the State University of New York at Binghamton, he was director of the Fernand Braudel Center for the Study of Economies, Historical Systems, and Civilizations.

Max Weber (1864–1920) was a German scholar of political economy and social science who is widely credited as one of the founders of modern sociology. His main interests were in the sociology of religion and economic sociology, which he combined in his best-known work, *The Protestant Ethic and the Spirit of Capitalism* (1905), on the relationship between Protestantism and the development of both Western capitalism and the nation-state.

WORKS CITED

WORKS CITED

Abu-Lughod, Ibrahim. "The Arab Rediscovery of Europe, 1800–1870." PhD diss., Princeton University, 1957.

The Arab Rediscovery of Europe: A Study in Cultural Encounters. Princeton, NJ: Princeton University Press, 1963.

Abu-Lughod, Janet L. "The Ecology of Cairo, Egypt: A Comparative Study using Factor Analysis." PhD diss., University of Massachusetts Amherst, 1966.

Cairo: 1001 Years of the City Victorious. Princeton, NJ: Princeton University Press, 1971.

Changing Cities: Urban Sociology. Glenview, IL: HarperCollins, 1991.

Rabat: Urban Apartheid in Morocco. Princeton, NJ: Princeton University Press, 1980.

Before European Hegemony: The World-System A.D. 1250–1350. Oxford: Oxford University Press, 1989.

"Restructuring the Premodern World-System." *Review* 13 (1990): 273–86.

"Going beyond Global Babble." In *Culture, Globalization and the World-System: Contemporary Conditions for the Representations of Identity*, edited by Anthony D. King, 131–7. Basingstoke: Macmillan, 1991.

"Reply to Donald Nielsen's 'After World Systems Theory'." *International Journal of Politics, Culture and Society* 4 (1991): 499–500.

"Comparing Chicago, New York, and Los Angeles: Testing Some World-cities Hypotheses." In *World-Cities in a World-System*, edited by Peter L. Knox and Peter J. Taylor, 171–91. Cambridge: Cambridge University Press, 1995.

"The World System Perspective in the Construction of Economic History." *History and Theory* 34 (1995): 86–98.

New York, Chicago, Los Angeles: America's Global Cities. Minneapolis: University of Minnesota Press, 1999.

"Lewis Mumford's Contributions to the History of Cities: A Critical Appraisal." Paper presented at first annual Lewis Mumford Lecture, University of Albany, New York, April 12, 2000.

Race, Space, and Riots in Chicago, New York, and Los Angeles. Oxford: Oxford University Press, 2007.

Abu-Lughod, Janet L., and Richard A. Hay, eds. *Third World Urbanization.* Chicago: Maaroufa Press, 1977.

Abu-Lughod, Janet L., et al. *From Urban Village to East Village: The Battle for New York's Lower East Side*. Oxford: Basil Blackwell UK, 1994.

Akihiko, Tanaka. *The New Middle Ages: The World System in the 21st Century*. Translated by Jean Connell Hoff. Tokyo: International House of Japan, 2002.

Balaev, Mikhail. "The Effects of International Trade on Democracy: A Panel Study of the Post-Soviet World-System." *Sociological Perspectives* 52 (2009): 337–62.

Beaujard, Philippe. "The Indian Ocean in Eurasian and African World-Systems before the Sixteenth Century." *Journal of World History* 16 (2005): 411–65.

Bentley, Jerry H. *Old World Encounters: Cross-Cultural Contacts and Exchanges in Pre-Modern Times.* Oxford: Oxford University Press, 1993.

"Cross-Cultural interaction and Periodization in World History." *American Historical Review* 101 (1996): 749–70.

Bergesen, Albert. "Pre vs. Post 1500ers." *Comparative Civilisations Review* 30 (1994): 81–9.

Blaut, James M. *1492: The Debate on Colonialism, Eurocentrism and History*. Trenton, NJ: Africa World Press, 1992.

Blomquist, Thomas W. "Review of Janet Abu-Lughod, *Before European Hegemony*." *Business History Review* 64 (1990): 362–4.

Bosworth, Andrew. "World-Cities and World Economic Cycles." In *Civilizations and World Systems: Studying World-Historical Change*, edited by Stephen K. Sanderson, 206–27. Walnut Creek, CA: Altamira Press, 1995.

Braudel, Fernand. *The Perspective of the World*. Vol. 3 of *Capitalism and Civilization, 15th–18th Century*. Translated by Sian Reynolds. London: William Collins, 1984.

Chase-Dunn, Christopher, and Thomas D. Hall. "Forward into the Past: World-Systems before 1500." *Sociological Forum* 9 (1994): 295–306.

Rise and Demise: Comparing World-Systems. Boulder, CO: Westview Press, 1997.

Chirot, Daniel. "Was Europe Lucky, Evil or Smart? Review of Janet Abu-Lughod, *Before European Hegemony*." *Comparative Sociology* 20 (1991): 26–8.

Clark, Rob. "World-System Mobility and Economic Growth, 1980–2000." *Social Forces* 88 (2010): 1123–51.

Curtin, Philip D. *Cross-Cultural Exchange in World History*. Cambridge: Cambridge University Press, 1984.

Del Cerro Santamaría, Gerardo. "Bilbao and Globalization: Transnational Networks, Political Economy, and Urban Restructuring in a City on the Global Map." PhD diss., New School for Social Research, 2003.

Ekholm, Kajsa, and Jonathan Friedman. "Capitalism, Imperialism and Exploitation in the Ancient World-Systems." *Review* 6 (1982): 87–110.

Frank, Andre Gunder. "The Thirteenth-Century World-System: A Review Essay." *Journal of World History* 1 (1990): 249–56.

ReOrient: Global Economy in the Asian Age. Berkeley: University of California Press, 1998.

Frank, Andre Gunder, and Barry K. Gills, eds. *The World System: Five Hundred Years or Five Thousand?* London: Routledge, 1993.

Friedmann, John, and Goetz Wolff. "World City Formation: An Agenda for Research and Action." *International Journal of Urban and Regional Research* 6, no. 3 (1982): 309–44.

Gernet, Jacques. *Daily Life in China on the Eve of the Mongol Invasion.* Translated by H. M. Wright. London: George Allen and Unwin, 1962.

Green, William A. "Periodisation in European and World History." *Journal of World History* 3 (1992): 13–53.

"Periodising World History." *History and Theory* 34 (1995): 99–111.

Grief, Avner. "Review of Janet Abu-Lughod, *Before European Hegemony*." *Journal of Economic History* 50 (1991): 455–6.

Hall, Thomas D., and Christopher Chase-Dunn. "Comparing World Systems: Concepts and Working Hypotheses." *Social Forces* 71 (1993): 851–86.

"Forward into the Past: World-Systems before 1500." *Sociological Forum* 9 (1994): 295–306.

Knox, P. L., and P. J. Taylor, eds. *World Cities in a World-System.* Cambridge: Cambridge University Press, 1995.

Kown, Roy. "Hegemonies in the World-System: An Empirical Assessment of Hegemonic Sequences from the 16th to 20th Century." *Sociological Perspectives* 54 (2011): 593–617.

Kuhn, Thomas S. *The Structure of Scientific Revolutions.* Chicago: University of Chicago Press, 1961.

Lewis, Archibald R. "Review of Janet Abu-Lughod, *Before European Hegemony*." *Speculum* 66 (1991): 605–06.

Lieberman, Victor. "Abu-Lughod's Egalitarian World Order: A Review Article." *Comparative Studies in Society and History* 35 (1993): 544–50.

Lombard, Maurice. *The Golden Age of Islam.* Translated by J. Spencer. Amsterdam: North-Holland, 1975.

Mann, Michael. *The Sources of Social Power*. Vol. 1 of *A History of Power from the Beginning to AD 1760*. Cambridge: Cambridge University Press, 1986.

Manz, Beatrice F. "Review of Janet Abu-Lughod, *Before European Hegemony*." *Journal of Interdisciplinary History* 22 (1991): 101–03.

Marx, Karl. *Pre-Capitalist Economic Formations*. Edited by Eric Hobsbawm. London: Lawrence & Wishart, 1964.

McNeill, William H. *The Rise of the West: A History of the Human Community*. Chicago: University of Chicago Press, 1963.

Mele, Christopher. "Reinventing the East Village of New York: Capitalist Investment Strategies, 1860–1990." PhD diss., New School for Social Research, 1994.

Mielants, Eric. *The Origins of Capitalism and the "Rise of the West."* Philadelphia: Temple University Press, 2007.

Moore III, Joseph Price. "Native Americans in Colonial New England and the Modern World-System." PhD diss., New Brunswick: Rutgers University Press, 2011.

Mumford, Lewis. *Technics and Civilisation*. London: Routledge and Kegan Paul, 1934.

The Culture of Cities. London: Secker & Warburg, 1938.

The City in History: Its Origins, its Transformations and its Prospects. London: Secker & Warburg Publishers, 1961.

Nielsen, Donald A. "After World Systems Theory: Concerning Janet Abu-Lughod's *Before European Hegemony*." *International Journal of Politics, Culture and Society* 4 (1991): 481–97.

Pirenne, Henri, *Medieval Cities: Their Origins and the Revival of Trade*. Translated by Frank D. Halsey. Princeton, NJ: Princeton University Press, 1925.

Mohammed and Charlemagne. Translated by Bernard Miall. London: Allen & Unwin, 1939.

Pollard, Elizabeth Ann. "Placing Greco-Roman History in World Historical Context." *The Classical World* 102 (2008): 53–68.

Pounds, Norman J. G. "Review of Janet Abu-Lughod, *Before European Hegemony*." *Annals of the Association of American Geographers* 81 (1991): 159–60.

Said, Edward. "Ibrahim Abu-Lughod." Guardian, June 12, 2001.

Sassen, Saskia. *Cities in a World Economy*. Thousand Oaks, CA: Pine Forge Press, 1994.

Schneider, Jane. "Was There a Pre-Capitalist World-System?" *Peasant Studies* 6 (1977): 20–7.

Sherman, Steven Marc. "Hegemonic Transitions and Cultural Change: The Making and Unmaking of Hegemonic Modernity in the Modern World System." PhD diss., State University of New York, 1999.

Shih, Miin-Wen. "The Rise of China in World-System Perspective." PhD diss., State University of New York, 2001.

Smith, Alan K. *Creating a World Economy: Merchant Capital, Colonialism and World Trade, 1400–1825.* Boulder, CO: Westview Press, 1991.

Toynbee, Arnold J. *A Study of History*, 12 vols. London: Oxford University Press, 1934–61.

Wallerstein, Immanuel M. *Capitalist Agriculture and the Origins of the European World-Economy in the sixteenth Century.* Vol. 1 of *The Modern World-System*. New York: Academic Press, 1974.

Mercantilism and the Consolidation of the European World-Economy, 1600–1750. Vol. 2 of *The Modern World-System*. New York: Academic Press, 1980.

The Second Era of Great Expansion of the Capitalist World-Economy, 1730–1840s. Vol. 3 of *The Modern World-System*. London: Academic Press, 1989.

"Review of Janet Abu-Lughod, *Before European Hegemony*." *International Journal of Middle East Studies* 24 (1992): 128–31.

Centrist Liberalism Triumphant, 1789–1914. Vol. 4 of *The Modern World-System*. Berkeley: University of California Press, 2011.

Weber, Max. *The Protestant Ethic and the Spirit of Capitalism*. Translated by Talcott Parsons. London: Allen & Unwin, 1930.

The City. Translated by Don Martindale and Gertrud Neuwirth. Glencoe, IL: Free Press, 1958.

Willard, Alice Louise. "Gold, Islam, and Camels: The Transformative Effects of Trade and Ideology." *Comparative Civilizations Review* 29 (1993): 80–105.

"Rivers of Gold, Oceans of Sand: The Songhay in the West African World-System." PhD diss., Johns Hopkins University, 1999.

THE MACAT LIBRARY
BY DISCIPLINE

The Macat Library By Discipline

AFRICANA STUDIES

Chinua Achebe's *An Image of Africa: Racism in Conrad's Heart of Darkness*
W. E. B. Du Bois's *The Souls of Black Folk*
Zora Neale Huston's *Characteristics of Negro Expression*
Martin Luther King Jr's *Why We Can't Wait*
Toni Morrison's *Playing in the Dark: Whiteness in the American Literary Imagination*

ANTHROPOLOGY

Arjun Appadurai's *Modernity at Large: Cultural Dimensions of Globalisation*
Philippe Ariès's *Centuries of Childhood*
Franz Boas's *Race, Language and Culture*
Kim Chan & Renée Mauborgne's *Blue Ocean Strategy*
Jared Diamond's *Guns, Germs & Steel: the Fate of Human Societies*
Jared Diamond's *Collapse: How Societies Choose to Fail or Survive*
E. E. Evans-Pritchard's *Witchcraft, Oracles and Magic Among the Azande*
James Ferguson's *The Anti-Politics Machine*
Clifford Geertz's *The Interpretation of Cultures*
David Graeber's *Debt: the First 5000 Years*
Karen Ho's *Liquidated: An Ethnography of Wall Street*
Geert Hofstede's *Culture's Consequences: Comparing Values, Behaviors, Institutes and Organizations across Nations*
Claude Lévi-Strauss's *Structural Anthropology*
Jay Macleod's *Ain't No Makin' It: Aspirations and Attainment in a Low-Income Neighborhood*
Saba Mahmood's *The Politics of Piety: The Islamic Revival and the Feminist Subjec*t
Marcel Mauss's *The Gift*

BUSINESS

Jean Lave & Etienne Wenger's *Situated Learning*
Theodore Levitt's *Marketing Myopia*
Burton G. Malkiel's *A Random Walk Down Wall Street*
Douglas McGregor's *The Human Side of Enterprise*
Michael Porter's *Competitive Strategy: Creating and Sustaining Superior Performance*
John Kotter's *Leading Change*
C. K. Prahalad & Gary Hamel's *The Core Competence of the Corporation*

CRIMINOLOGY

Michelle Alexander's *The New Jim Crow: Mass Incarceration in the Age of Colorblindness*
Michael R. Gottfredson & Travis Hirschi's *A General Theory of Crime*
Richard Herrnstein & Charles A. Murray's *The Bell Curve: Intelligence and Class Structure in American Life*
Elizabeth Loftus's *Eyewitness Testimony*
Jay Macleod's *Ain't No Makin' It: Aspirations and Attainment in a Low-Income Neighborhood*
Philip Zimbardo's *The Lucifer Effect*

ECONOMICS

Janet Abu-Lughod's *Before European Hegemony*
Ha-Joon Chang's *Kicking Away the Ladder*
David Brion Davis's *The Problem of Slavery in the Age of Revolution*
Milton Friedman's *The Role of Monetary Policy*
Milton Friedman's *Capitalism and Freedom*
David Graeber's *Debt: the First 5000 Years*
Friedrich Hayek's *The Road to Serfdom*
Karen Ho's *Liquidated: An Ethnography of Wall Street*

John Maynard Keynes's *The General Theory of Employment, Interest and Money*
Charles P. Kindleberger's *Manias, Panics and Crashes*
Robert Lucas's *Why Doesn't Capital Flow from Rich to Poor Countries?*
Burton G. Malkiel's *A Random Walk Down Wall Street*
Thomas Robert Malthus's *An Essay on the Principle of Population*
Karl Marx's *Capital*
Thomas Piketty's *Capital in the Twenty-First Century*
Amartya Sen's *Development as Freedom*
Adam Smith's *The Wealth of Nations*
Nassim Nicholas Taleb's *The Black Swan: The Impact of the Highly Improbable*
Amos Tversky's & Daniel Kahneman's *Judgment under Uncertainty: Heuristics and Biases*
Mahbub Ul Haq's *Reflections on Human Development*
Max Weber's *The Protestant Ethic and the Spirit of Capitalism*

FEMINISM AND GENDER STUDIES

Judith Butler's *Gender Trouble*
Simone De Beauvoir's *The Second Sex*
Michel Foucault's *History of Sexuality*
Betty Friedan's *The Feminine Mystique*
Saba Mahmood's *The Politics of Piety: The Islamic Revival and the Feminist Subject*
Joan Wallach Scott's *Gender and the Politics of History*
Mary Wollstonecraft's *A Vindication of the Rights of Woman*
Virginia Woolf's *A Room of One's Own*

GEOGRAPHY

The Brundtland Report's *Our Common Future*
Rachel Carson's *Silent Spring*
Charles Darwin's *On the Origin of Species*
James Ferguson's *The Anti-Politics Machine*
Jane Jacobs's *The Death and Life of Great American Cities*
James Lovelock's *Gaia: A New Look at Life on Earth*
Amartya Sen's *Development as Freedom*
Mathis Wackernagel & William Rees's *Our Ecological Footprint*

HISTORY

Janet Abu-Lughod's *Before European Hegemony*
Benedict Anderson's *Imagined Communities*
Bernard Bailyn's *The Ideological Origins of the American Revolution*
Hanna Batatu's *The Old Social Classes And The Revolutionary Movements Of Iraq*
Christopher Browning's *Ordinary Men: Reserve Police Batallion 101 and the Final Solution in Poland*
Edmund Burke's *Reflections on the Revolution in France*
William Cronon's *Nature's Metropolis: Chicago And The Great West*
Alfred W. Crosby's *The Columbian Exchange*
Hamid Dabashi's *Iran: A People Interrupted*
David Brion Davis's *The Problem of Slavery in the Age of Revolution*
Nathalie Zemon Davis's *The Return of Martin Guerre*
Jared Diamond's *Guns, Germs & Steel: the Fate of Human Societies*
Frank Dikotter's *Mao's Great Famine*
John W Dower's *War Without Mercy: Race And Power In The Pacific War*
W. E. B. Du Bois's *The Souls of Black Folk*
Richard J. Evans's *In Defence of History*
Lucien Febvre's *The Problem of Unbelief in the 16th Century*
Sheila Fitzpatrick's *Everyday Stalinism*

The Macat Library By Discipline

Eric Foner's *Reconstruction: America's Unfinished Revolution, 1863-1877*
Michel Foucault's *Discipline and Punish*
Michel Foucault's *History of Sexuality*
Francis Fukuyama's *The End of History and the Last Man*
John Lewis Gaddis's *We Now Know: Rethinking Cold War History*
Ernest Gellner's *Nations and Nationalism*
Eugene Genovese's *Roll, Jordan, Roll: The World the Slaves Made*
Carlo Ginzburg's *The Night Battles*
Daniel Goldhagen's *Hitler's Willing Executioners*
Jack Goldstone's *Revolution and Rebellion in the Early Modern World*
Antonio Gramsci's *The Prison Notebooks*
Alexander Hamilton, John Jay & James Madison's *The Federalist Papers*
Christopher Hill's *The World Turned Upside Down*
Carole Hillenbrand's *The Crusades: Islamic Perspectives*
Thomas Hobbes's *Leviathan*
Eric Hobsbawm's *The Age Of Revolution*
John A. Hobson's *Imperialism: A Study*
Albert Hourani's *History of the Arab Peoples*
Samuel P. Huntington's *The Clash of Civilizations and the Remaking of World Order*
C. L. R. James's *The Black Jacobins*
Tony Judt's *Postwar: A History of Europe Since 1945*
Ernst Kantorowicz's *The King's Two Bodies: A Study in Medieval Political Theology*
Paul Kennedy's *The Rise and Fall of the Great Powers*
Ian Kershaw's *The "Hitler Myth": Image and Reality in the Third Reich*
John Maynard Keynes's *The General Theory of Employment, Interest and Money*
Charles P. Kindleberger's *Manias, Panics and Crashes*
Martin Luther King Jr's *Why We Can't Wait*
Henry Kissinger's *World Order: Reflections on the Character of Nations and the Course of History*
Thomas Kuhn's *The Structure of Scientific Revolutions*
Georges Lefebvre's *The Coming of the French Revolution*
John Locke's *Two Treatises of Government*
Niccolò Machiavelli's *The Prince*
Thomas Robert Malthus's *An Essay on the Principle of Population*
Mahmood Mamdani's *Citizen and Subject: Contemporary Africa And The Legacy Of Late Colonialism*
Karl Marx's *Capital*
Stanley Milgram's *Obedience to Authority*
John Stuart Mill's *On Liberty*
Thomas Paine's *Common Sense*
Thomas Paine's *Rights of Man*
Geoffrey Parker's *Global Crisis: War, Climate Change and Catastrophe in the Seventeenth Century*
Jonathan Riley-Smith's *The First Crusade and the Idea of Crusading*
Jean-Jacques Rousseau's *The Social Contract*
Joan Wallach Scott's *Gender and the Politics of History*
Theda Skocpol's *States and Social Revolutions*
Adam Smith's *The Wealth of Nations*
Timothy Snyder's *Bloodlands: Europe Between Hitler and Stalin*
Sun Tzu's *The Art of War*
Keith Thomas's *Religion and the Decline of Magic*
Thucydides's *The History of the Peloponnesian War*
Frederick Jackson Turner's *The Significance of the Frontier in American History*
Odd Arne Westad's *The Global Cold War: Third World Interventions And The Making Of Our Times*

LITERATURE

Chinua Achebe's *An Image of Africa: Racism in Conrad's Heart of Darkness*
Roland Barthes's *Mythologies*
Homi K. Bhabha's *The Location of Culture*
Judith Butler's *Gender Trouble*
Simone De Beauvoir's *The Second Sex*
Ferdinand De Saussure's *Course in General Linguistics*
T. S. Eliot's *The Sacred Wood: Essays on Poetry and Criticism*
Zora Neale Huston's *Characteristics of Negro Expression*
Toni Morrison's *Playing in the Dark: Whiteness in the American Literary Imagination*
Edward Said's *Orientalism*
Gayatri Chakravorty Spivak's *Can the Subaltern Speak?*
Mary Wollstonecraft's *A Vindication of the Rights of Women*
Virginia Woolf's *A Room of One's Own*

PHILOSOPHY

Elizabeth Anscombe's *Modern Moral Philosophy*
Hannah Arendt's *The Human Condition*
Aristotle's *Metaphysics*
Aristotle's *Nicomachean Ethics*
Edmund Gettier's *Is Justified True Belief Knowledge?*
Georg Wilhelm Friedrich Hegel's *Phenomenology of Spirit*
David Hume's *Dialogues Concerning Natural Religion*
David Hume's *The Enquiry for Human Understanding*
Immanuel Kant's *Religion within the Boundaries of Mere Reason*
Immanuel Kant's *Critique of Pure Reason*
Søren Kierkegaard's *The Sickness Unto Death*
Søren Kierkegaard's *Fear and Trembling*
C. S. Lewis's *The Abolition of Man*
Alasdair MacIntyre's *After Virtue*
Marcus Aurelius's *Meditations*
Friedrich Nietzsche's *On the Genealogy of Morality*
Friedrich Nietzsche's *Beyond Good and Evil*
Plato's *Republic*
Plato's *Symposium*
Jean-Jacques Rousseau's *The Social Contract*
Gilbert Ryle's *The Concept of Mind*
Baruch Spinoza's *Ethics*
Sun Tzu's *The Art of War*
Ludwig Wittgenstein's *Philosophical Investigations*

POLITICS

Benedict Anderson's *Imagined Communities*
Aristotle's *Politics*
Bernard Bailyn's *The Ideological Origins of the American Revolution*
Edmund Burke's *Reflections on the Revolution in France*
John C. Calhoun's *A Disquisition on Government*
Ha-Joon Chang's *Kicking Away the Ladder*
Hamid Dabashi's *Iran: A People Interrupted*
Hamid Dabashi's *Theology of Discontent: The Ideological Foundation of the Islamic Revolution in Iran*
Robert Dahl's *Democracy and its Critics*
Robert Dahl's *Who Governs?*
David Brion Davis's *The Problem of Slavery in the Age of Revolution*

The Macat Library By Discipline

Alexis De Tocqueville's *Democracy in America*
James Ferguson's *The Anti-Politics Machine*
Frank Dikotter's *Mao's Great Famine*
Sheila Fitzpatrick's *Everyday Stalinism*
Eric Foner's *Reconstruction: America's Unfinished Revolution, 1863-1877*
Milton Friedman's *Capitalism and Freedom*
Francis Fukuyama's *The End of History and the Last Man*
John Lewis Gaddis's *We Now Know: Rethinking Cold War History*
Ernest Gellner's *Nations and Nationalism*
David Graeber's *Debt: the First 5000 Years*
Antonio Gramsci's *The Prison Notebooks*
Alexander Hamilton, John Jay & James Madison's *The Federalist Papers*
Friedrich Hayek's *The Road to Serfdom*
Christopher Hill's *The World Turned Upside Down*
Thomas Hobbes's *Leviathan*
John A. Hobson's *Imperialism: A Study*
Samuel P. Huntington's *The Clash of Civilizations and the Remaking of World Order*
Tony Judt's *Postwar: A History of Europe Since 1945*
David C. Kang's *China Rising: Peace, Power and Order in East Asia*
Paul Kennedy's *The Rise and Fall of Great Powers*
Robert Keohane's *After Hegemony*
Martin Luther King Jr.'s *Why We Can't Wait*
Henry Kissinger's *World Order: Reflections on the Character of Nations and the Course of History*
John Locke's *Two Treatises of Government*
Niccolò Machiavelli's *The Prince*
Thomas Robert Malthus's *An Essay on the Principle of Population*
Mahmood Mamdani's *Citizen and Subject: Contemporary Africa And The Legacy Of Late Colonialism*
Karl Marx's *Capital*
John Stuart Mill's *On Liberty*
John Stuart Mill's *Utilitarianism*
Hans Morgenthau's *Politics Among Nations*
Thomas Paine's *Common Sense*
Thomas Paine's *Rights of Man*
Thomas Piketty's *Capital in the Twenty-First Century*
Robert D. Putman's *Bowling Alone*
John Rawls's *Theory of Justice*
Jean-Jacques Rousseau's *The Social Contract*
Theda Skocpol's *States and Social Revolutions*
Adam Smith's *The Wealth of Nations*
Sun Tzu's *The Art of War*
Henry David Thoreau's *Civil Disobedience*
Thucydides's *The History of the Peloponnesian War*
Kenneth Waltz's *Theory of International Politics*
Max Weber's *Politics as a Vocation*
Odd Arne Westad's *The Global Cold War: Third World Interventions And The Making Of Our Times*

POSTCOLONIAL STUDIES

Roland Barthes's *Mythologies*
Frantz Fanon's *Black Skin, White Masks*
Homi K. Bhabha's *The Location of Culture*
Gustavo Gutiérrez's *A Theology of Liberation*
Edward Said's *Orientalism*
Gayatri Chakravorty Spivak's *Can the Subaltern Speak?*

PSYCHOLOGY

Gordon Allport's *The Nature of Prejudice*
Alan Baddeley & Graham Hitch's *Aggression: A Social Learning Analysis*
Albert Bandura's *Aggression: A Social Learning Analysis*
Leon Festinger's *A Theory of Cognitive Dissonance*
Sigmund Freud's *The Interpretation of Dreams*
Betty Friedan's *The Feminine Mystique*
Michael R. Gottfredson & Travis Hirschi's *A General Theory of Crime*
Eric Hoffer's *The True Believer: Thoughts on the Nature of Mass Movements*
William James's *Principles of Psychology*
Elizabeth Loftus's *Eyewitness Testimony*
A. H. Maslow's *A Theory of Human Motivation*
Stanley Milgram's *Obedience to Authority*
Steven Pinker's *The Better Angels of Our Nature*
Oliver Sacks's *The Man Who Mistook His Wife For a Hat*
Richard Thaler & Cass Sunstein's *Nudge: Improving Decisions About Health, Wealth and Happiness*
Amos Tversky's *Judgment under Uncertainty: Heuristics and Biases*
Philip Zimbardo's *The Lucifer Effect*

SCIENCE

Rachel Carson's *Silent Spring*
William Cronon's *Nature's Metropolis: Chicago And The Great West*
Alfred W. Crosby's *The Columbian Exchange*
Charles Darwin's *On the Origin of Species*
Richard Dawkin's *The Selfish Gene*
Thomas Kuhn's *The Structure of Scientific Revolutions*
Geoffrey Parker's *Global Crisis: War, Climate Change and Catastrophe in the Seventeenth Century*
Mathis Wackernagel & William Rees's *Our Ecological Footprint*

SOCIOLOGY

Michelle Alexander's *The New Jim Crow: Mass Incarceration in the Age of Colorblindness*
Gordon Allport's *The Nature of Prejudice*
Albert Bandura's *Aggression: A Social Learning Analysis*
Hanna Batatu's *The Old Social Classes And The Revolutionary Movements Of Iraq*
Ha-Joon Chang's *Kicking Away the Ladder*
W. E. B. Du Bois's *The Souls of Black Folk*
Émile Durkheim's *On Suicide*
Frantz Fanon's *Black Skin, White Masks*
Frantz Fanon's *The Wretched of the Earth*
Eric Foner's *Reconstruction: America's Unfinished Revolution, 1863-1877*
Eugene Genovese's *Roll, Jordan, Roll: The World the Slaves Made*
Jack Goldstone's *Revolution and Rebellion in the Early Modern World*
Antonio Gramsci's *The Prison Notebooks*
Richard Herrnstein & Charles A Murray's *The Bell Curve: Intelligence and Class Structure in American Life*
Eric Hoffer's *The True Believer: Thoughts on the Nature of Mass Movements*
Jane Jacobs's *The Death and Life of Great American Cities*
Robert Lucas's *Why Doesn't Capital Flow from Rich to Poor Countries?*
Jay Macleod's *Ain't No Makin' It: Aspirations and Attainment in a Low Income Neighborhood*
Elaine May's *Homeward Bound: American Families in the Cold War Era*
Douglas McGregor's *The Human Side of Enterprise*
C. Wright Mills's *The Sociological Imagination*

The Macat Library By Discipline

Thomas Piketty's *Capital in the Twenty-First Century*
Robert D. Putman's *Bowling Alone*
David Riesman's *The Lonely Crowd: A Study of the Changing American Character*
Edward Said's *Orientalism*
Joan Wallach Scott's *Gender and the Politics of History*
Theda Skocpol's *States and Social Revolutions*
Max Weber's *The Protestant Ethic and the Spirit of Capitalism*

THEOLOGY

Augustine's *Confessions*
Benedict's *Rule of St Benedict*
Gustavo Gutiérrez's *A Theology of Liberation*
Carole Hillenbrand's *The Crusades: Islamic Perspectives*
David Hume's *Dialogues Concerning Natural Religion*
Immanuel Kant's *Religion within the Boundaries of Mere Reason*
Ernst Kantorowicz's *The King's Two Bodies: A Study in Medieval Political Theology*
Søren Kierkegaard's *The Sickness Unto Death*
C. S. Lewis's *The Abolition of Man*
Saba Mahmood's *The Politics of Piety: The Islamic Revival and the Feminist Subject*
Baruch Spinoza's *Ethics*
Keith Thomas's *Religion and the Decline of Magic*

COMING SOON

Chris Argyris's *The Individual and the Organisation*
Seyla Benhabib's *The Rights of Others*
Walter Benjamin's *The Work Of Art in the Age of Mechanical Reproduction*
John Berger's *Ways of Seeing*
Pierre Bourdieu's *Outline of a Theory of Practice*
Mary Douglas's *Purity and Danger*
Roland Dworkin's *Taking Rights Seriously*
James G. March's *Exploration and Exploitation in Organisational Learning*
Ikujiro Nonaka's *A Dynamic Theory of Organizational Knowledge Creation*
Griselda Pollock's *Vision and Difference*
Amartya Sen's *Inequality Re-Examined*
Susan Sontag's *On Photography*
Yasser Tabbaa's *The Transformation of Islamic Art*
Ludwig von Mises's *Theory of Money and Credit*

Macat Disciplines

Access the greatest ideas and thinkers across entire disciplines, including

Postcolonial Studies

Roland Barthes's *Mythologies*
Frantz Fanon's *Black Skin, White Masks*
Homi K. Bhabha's *The Location of Culture*
Gustavo Gutiérrez's *A Theology of Liberation*
Edward Said's *Orientalism*
Gayatri Chakravorty Spivak's *Can the Subaltern Speak?*

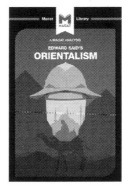

Macat analyses are available from all good bookshops and libraries.

Access hundreds of analyses through one, multimedia tool.
Join free for one month **library.macat.com**

Macat Pairs

Analyse historical and modern issues from opposite sides of an argument. Pairs include:

ARE WE FUNDAMENTALLY GOOD - OR BAD?

Steven Pinker's
The Better Angels of Our Nature

Stephen Pinker's gloriously optimistic 2011 book argues that, despite humanity's biological tendency toward violence, we are, in fact, less violent today than ever before. To prove his case, Pinker lays out pages of detailed statistical evidence. For him, much of the credit for the decline goes to the eighteenth-century Enlightenment movement, whose ideas of liberty, tolerance, and respect for the value of human life filtered down through society and affected how people thought. That psychological change led to behavioral change—and overall we became more peaceful. Critics countered that humanity could never overcome the biological urge toward violence; others argued that Pinker's statistics were flawed.

Philip Zimbardo's
The Lucifer Effect

Some psychologists believe those who commit cruelty are innately evil. Zimbardo disagrees. In *The Lucifer Effect*, he argues that sometimes good people do evil things simply because of the situations they find themselves in, citing many historical examples to illustrate his point. Zimbardo details his 1971 Stanford prison experiment, where ordinary volunteers playing guards in a mock prison rapidly became abusive. But he also describes the tortures committed by US army personnel in Iraq's Abu Ghraib prison in 2003—and how he himself testified in defence of one of those guards. committed by US army personnel in Iraq's Abu Ghraib prison in 2003—and how he himself testified in defence of one of those guards.

Macat Pairs

Analyse historical and modern issues from opposite sides of an argument. Pairs include:

RACE AND IDENTITY

Zora Neale Hurston's
Characteristics of Negro Expression

Using material collected on anthropological expeditions to the South, Zora Neale Hurston explains how expression in African American culture in the early twentieth century departs from the art of white America. At the time, African American art was often criticized for copying white culture. For Hurston, this criticism misunderstood how art works. European tradition views art as something fixed. But Hurston describes a creative process that is alive, ever-changing, and largely improvisational. She maintains that African American art works through a process called 'mimicry'—where an imitated object or verbal pattern, for example, is reshaped and altered until it becomes something new, novel—and worthy of attention.

Frantz Fanon's
Black Skin, White Masks

Black Skin, White Masks offers a radical analysis of the psychological effects of colonization on the colonized.

Fanon witnessed the effects of colonization first hand both in his birthplace, Martinique, and again later in life when he worked as a psychiatrist in another French colony, Algeria. His text is uncompromising in form and argument. He dissects the dehumanizing effects of colonialism, arguing that it destroys the native sense of identity, forcing people to adapt to an alien set of values—including a core belief that they are inferior. This results in deep psychological trauma.

Fanon's work played a pivotal role in the civil rights movements of the 1960s.

Macat analyses are available from all good bookshops and libraries.

Access hundreds of analyses through one, multimedia tool.
Join free for one month **library.macat.com**

Macat Disciplines

Access the greatest ideas and thinkers across entire disciplines, including

INEQUALITY

Ha-Joon Chang's, *Kicking Away the Ladder*

David Graeber's, *Debt: The First 5000 Years*

Robert E. Lucas's, *Why Doesn't Capital Flow from Rich To Poor Countries?*

Thomas Piketty's, *Capital in the Twenty-First Century*

Amartya Sen's, *Inequality Re-Examined*

Mahbub Ul Haq's, *Reflections on Human Development*

Macat analyses are available from all good bookshops and libraries.

Access hundreds of analyses through one, multimedia tool.
Join free for one month **library.macat.com**

Printed in the United States
by Baker & Taylor Publisher Services